The Revelation to John

The Revelation to John

A Commentary

Martin H. Franzmann

Publishing House
St. Louis

Write the vision;
    make it plain upon tablets,
    so he who runs may read it.
For still the vision waits its time;
    it hastens to the end—it will not lie.
If it seem slow, wait for it;
    it will surely come, it will not delay.

Hab. 2:2-3

Copyright 1968 Concordia Publishing House
3558 S. Jefferson Avenue
St. Louis, Missouri 63118
Revised edition 1975
MANUFACTURED IN THE UNITED STATES OF AMERICA

Library of Congress Catloging-in-Publication data

Franzmann, Martin H.
    The Revelation to John.

    Bibliography: p.
    1. Bible. N.T. Revelation—Commentaries. I. Title.
BS2825.3.F68   1986   228'.07   86-927
ISBN 0-570-04430-8

        7 8 9 10   96 95 94 93

Contents

INTRODUCTION
TO THE BOOK

Martin Luther in the Preface to his translation of the New Testament of 1522 complained concerning The Revelation to John: "My spirit cannot adapt itself to the book." He stated expressly that he did not wish to bind anyone else to his judgment, leaving it free to each man to judge of the book as that man's spirit dictated to him; but he relegated it (together with Hebrews, James, Jude) to a sort of appendix, did not number its pages with the rest, and he gave his reasons for so doing. The reasons were chiefly two, one substantive and one formal.

The substantive reason he expresses thus:

> For me it is reason enough for not esteeming it highly that in it Christ is neither taught nor recognized, which is, above all, an apostle's business, as He says Acts 1:8: "You shall be my witnesses." Therefore I stay with the books which proffer Christ to me clearly and purely.

The formal reason, given first, he states as follows:

> I say what I feel. I have more than one reason for declining to consider this book either apostolic or prophetic. First and foremost, the apostles do not occupy themselves with visions but prophesy with clear, crisp words, as Peter, Paul, and Christ in the gospels also do; for it befits the apostolic office to speak clearly, without image and without visions of Christ and His work.

Luther was not the first to have difficulty with the last book of the Bible; he himself notes that "many of the fathers rejected the book of old, though St. Jerome uses high language and says that it is above all praise." Dionysius of Alexandria in the third century, for example, noting that before his time some had completely rejected the book as unclear, lacking in clear connection, and even heretical, will not make bold to reject the book but confesses that he can make nothing of it and is content to admire it reverently from a distance, as it were. Nor was Luther the last; though

7

Revelation has always had its admirers and even its fanatical devotees and has left its mark indelibly on the art and song of the church, yet it has remained for many a puzzling, cryptic sort of writing, not clearly or closely related to the central Gospel of the New Testament. Reactions to Revelation still range all the way from a respectful reserve over against it to distaste and all-but-rejection, practically if not in principle. If we are not to join the ranks either of the fanatical devotees or of those who reject or neglect it, we shall do well to consider the questions raised by Martin Luther (he has, as so often, come close to the heart of the matter) and so come closer perhaps to a genuine understanding and appreciation of the book:

A. Is Revelation, in substance, so remote from the heart of the New Testament Gospel that it is practically irrelevant for the church of today and tomorrow?
B. Is Revelation, in form, so strange, bizarre, and undisciplined that we can find no real access to it? (As Luther put it in his Preface: "They are to be blessed who keep what is written therein [1:3], and yet no one knows what that is, to say nothing of being able to keep it; so that it amounts to the same thing as not having at all what is in the book.")

It may be well to recall, at the outset, that Luther wrote another Preface to Revelation 23 years later (1545), whose moderated judgment and warmer appreciation is an indication both of the value of experience, not least bitter experience, for an understanding of this prophetic word and of the inherent vitality of the prophetic word itself, which so grew upon Luther that he not only radically revised his Preface to it but was moved by it to write a hymn on a theme suggested by it ("Sie ist mir lieb, die werte Magd," Rev. 12).

A. Luther's Substantive Objection: The Gospel in The Revelation to John

Luther's judgment concerning The Revelation to John (that in it "Christ is neither taught nor recognized" and that the book is therefore not a truly apostolic writing) is an astonishing one, coming as it does from one so sensitive to the centrality of the cross in the proclamation of Christ as Luther was. For whatever difficulties The Revelation to John may pose, there is surely no difficulty in recognizing that its proclamation of Christ is in the mainstream of the New Testament proclamation of Him as the Crucified.

When Paul says, "I decided to know nothing among you except Jesus Christ and him crucified" (1 Cor. 2:2; cf. Gal. 3:1), he is not speaking of an especially "slanted" or even abridged form of the Gospel; he is making a compendious statement of the totality of the Gospel. His proclamation of the Gospel in 1 Corinthians itself makes this plain. When he comes to speak, for instance, of the resurrection, he speaks of it as the completion of God's atoning act on the cross (1 Cor. 15:3, 17, 54); and he sees in the cross and the Crucified the answer to all the questions which troubled the church in Corinth. When the faith of the church threatened to fasten on the greatness of a man (whether Apollos, Cephas, or Paul himself), Paul points to the Crucified as the sole Lord of the church: "Is Christ divided? Was Paul crucified for you?" (1 Cor. 1:13). He will not tolerate a Gospel which empties "the cross of Christ of its power" by substituting for the cross of Christ an "eloquent wisdom" of men (1 Cor. 1:17). The cross, which pronounces an annihilating judgment on all human greatness and on all human wisdom, cuts off all human boasting of man and marks as monstrous and unnatural any clustering about great men in factions that give their loyalty to men. To men proud of possessing the Spirit and inclined to foster a spirituality which can disregard man's body and feed man's religious ego, Paul proclaims a spirituality rooted in the Cross, in that redeeming event in which the Son of God suffered in the flesh for men in the flesh, the event in which God spoke His Yea to the body which He had created. Paul therefore proclaims the Spirit who dwells in human bodies and lays a consecrating claim on them (1 Cor. 6:19). He proclaims the Spirit who enables men to call Jesus, the Accursed who hung upon the tree, Lord. (1 Cor. 12:3)

To men proud of wisdom which makes them "wise in this age" (1 Cor. 3:18), Paul proclaims the offensive wisdom of the cross (1 Cor. 2:6-13). Faced with a celebration of the Lord's

Supper which threatens to become a scene of carousing, the expression of man's contemptuous and divisive self-will, Paul reminds the church that this is the *Lord's* Supper, given by the Crucified "on the night when he was betrayed" (1 Cor. 11:23-26), to serve the living, enacted remembrance of His death for men's sins upon the cross. Throughout, Paul speaks both the indicative and the enabling creative imperative of the Gospel of the cross.

The indicative and the imperative Gospel of the cross is the theme of the gospels also. The indicative: The men who

> . . . found grace to pen
> The life which was the Life of men,

the authors of the gospels, penned strange biographies. The gospels have been aptly called "Passion stories with a preface." The amount of space allotted by the evangelists to the accounts of Jesus' suffering and death already bears witness to that, to say nothing of the many features throughout the gospel accounts which mark Jesus as the Man bound for the cross and the resurrection. The story of the life which was the Life of men is the story of a life given into a foreseen and willed death for men and their salvation.

The indicative of the Gospel as proclaimed in the gospels is the it-is-done of the Cross, the fact that "Christ died for our sins in accordance with the scriptures" according to the common apostolic Gospel which Paul proclaimed (before our gospels were written) as "of first importance" (1 Cor. 15:3; cf. 15:11). The Gospel imperative lies in the "Follow me" with which Jesus began the gathering of His disciples, His new Israel (Matt. 4:19, 22). It becomes increasingly apparent as the Good News is told, that to follow Jesus is to follow Him to the cross. When Matthew first portrays Jesus as teaching His disciples, Jesus calls His disciples blessed and inheritors of the Kingdom as men "persecuted for righteousness' sake," that is, for His sake (Matt. 5:10-12). Of all the beatitudes, the beatitude on the persecuted is particularly accented. The feet of the disciples are from the first set on paths of suffering. The key-signature of their ministering lives is the cross, as is but natural and inevitable for men whose only power lies in prayer (Matt. 7:7) and in love. (Matt. 7:12; cf. 5:43-48)

When Jesus sent 12 disciples as His apostles to the lost sheep of the house of Israel with the proclaimed and enacted good news of the kingdom-at-hand (Matt. 10:5-8), He imprinted the sign of the cross on their apostolate; sent out "as sheep in the midst of wolves" (Matt. 10:16), as maligned emissaries of a maligned Lord (Matt. 10:25), as the committed followers of One who brings no cheap popular peace on earth but a sword (Matt. 10:34-37), they have need of their Lord's "Fear not!" (Matt. 10:26, 28, 31) to sustain them under His stern promise: "He who does not take his cross and follow me is not worthy of me. He who finds his life will lose it, and he who loses his life for my sake will find it" (Matt. 10:38-39). The apostle marches under the royal banner of the cross.

The Christ puts His church under the cross when He promises Peter that the church He will build will be a church against which "the powers of death shall not prevail" (Matt. 16:18). The men gathered round the Christ by Peter and his fellow apostles will be men who take up their cross and die. No matter; their dying will not be defeat and death; it will be life and victory. The promise which sustains the apostle who denies himself and takes his cross to follow Christ (Matt. 16:24) will sustain the apostolic church in the hour of death and assure her a life beyond death when "the Son of man is to come with His angels in the glory of His Father and . . . will repay every man for what he has done." (Matt. 16:27)

It was the crucified and risen Lord, endowed with all authority in heaven and on earth, who bade His disciples: "Go therefore and make disciples of all nations" (Matt. 28:19), by baptizing them in His name with the baptism which commits them to His death and removes them into His life (Rom. 6:2-13) and by teaching them all that He had commanded them. "Making disciples" of the men of all nations involves both the indicative of the Gospel and the imperative of the Gospel; to conceive of the imperative merely as something that we colorlessly call "ethical teaching" is to fall short of what Jesus meant when He spoke of what "I have commanded you." We cannot but think of His prime imperatives, to which all ethical imperatives are related and subordinated: Follow Me . . . deny yourselves . . . take your cross . . . lose your life for My sake and gain life.

When the risen Christ, "alive after his passion" (Acts 1:3), gathered round Him again the disciples whom He had forgiven and restored after their failure at His cross, He once more bade them follow Him—to the cross. He told them: "You shall be my witnesses in Jerusalem and in all Judea and Samaria and to the end of the earth" (Acts 1:8). To be a witness to Christ is to be an all-out witness, to the death, a witness such as the Crucified Himself was, to the death (cf. John 18:37). Indeed, the Greek word for "witness" (*martys*) gave us our word "martyr." In Acts, Paul calls Stephen a "witness" of Christ as one whose blood was shed in testimony to the Lord (Acts 22:20); and in The Revelation to John, Antipas is called a faithful witness because he died at Pergamum rather than deny his faith. (2:13)

When the Lord made Paul His witness, "a chosen instrument to carry" His "name before the Gentiles and kings and the sons of Israel," He left no doubt that Paul was to be "witness" in the full martyr-sense: "I will show him how much he must *suffer* for the sake of my name" (Acts 9:15-16). To the end of his days Paul maintained that suffering was essential to his apostolate. "For this gospel I was appointed . . . apostle . . . and therefore I suffer as I do" (2 Tim. 1:11-12). Suffering is essential to his apostolate; it is also a validation of his apostolic Gospel: "Now you have observed my teaching . . . what persecutions I endured . . . . As for you, continue in what you have learned . . . knowing from whom you learned it" (2 Tim. 3:10-11, 14). The apostolic church, created by the Gospel of the cross, was marked by the Gospel of the cross as destined to remain the church under the cross, the *ecclesia sub cruce tecta,* as Luther puts it; "Through many tribulations we must enter the kingdom of God." (Acts 14:22)

Jesus' beatitude upon those persecuted for His sake (Matt. 5:10-12) was not forgotten in the apostolic church. It was remembered when the Gospel of the Crucified collided with the authorities of Judaism. When the Sanhedrin charged Peter and John "not to speak or teach at all in the name of Jesus" (Acts 4:18), the name of the Crucified raised from the dead by God (Acts 4:10-12), the apostles answered, "We cannot but speak of what we have seen and heard" (Acts

12

4:20). Then there began that irresistible and irreversible rhythm of hearing-and-telling which is the mark and the inner life of the church in witness to the Crucified. The joy of the crucified Lord is in His witnesses, and that is joy which no man can take away (cf. John 15:11; 16:22). Flogged and forbidden to speak, the witnessing apostles left the council of their persecutors "rejoicing that they were counted worthy to suffer dishonor for the name. And every day in the temple and at home they did not cease teaching and preaching Jesus as the Christ." (Acts 5:41-42)

When the persecution which began with the stoning of Stephen broke out and Saul (Paul), "breathing threats and murder" against the saints (Acts 9:1), made his systematic attack upon the church of God (cf. Gal. 1:13), the Spirit led men to see (as Luke's account in Acts shows, Acts 6:8—8:3) in Stephen one who heard his Lord's "Follow me" and was following Him whither He led. Like Him, Stephen was falsely accused by his enemies (Acts 6:11-14); like Him, he appealed in justification to the Old Testament (Acts 7:1-53); like Him, he commended his spirit, dying, into the hands of the Lord whom he served (Acts 7:59); like Him, he was able to look beyond death into life and glory (Acts 7:55-56); and like Him, he interceded for those responsible for his death (Acts 7:60). As the Jews demanded the death of Jesus from reluctant Pilate in the name of their law: "We have a law, and by that law he ought to die" (John 19:7), so at the death of Stephen the Law had its champion. Saul, zealous for the Law and the traditions of his fathers (Gal. 1:14), "was consenting to his death." (Acts 8:1)

But the Law and the men of the Law could not quench the witness of those who followed the Crucified; persecution brought home to the church the truth of Jesus' words: "They will deliver you up to councils . . . and the gospel *must* first be preached to all nations" (Mark 13:9-10). The "great persecution . . . against the church in Jerusalem" (Acts 8:1) scattered the men who had heard the Gospel of the Crucified and could not but speak it "throughout the region of Judea and Samaria" (Acts 8:1) and "as far as Phoenicia and Cyprus and Antioch" (Acts 11:19) and so, through Paul, turned witness to the Crucified, to Asia Minor and Europe. The

13

Gospel, they found, is a viscous liquid which will not disintegrate under pressure but spreads under pressure. The same divine "must" which carried Jesus to the cross (Matt. 16:21) carried the Gospel of the Crucified "to the end of the earth." (Acts 1:8)

Paul was not the last man in Jewry to attempt "to kick against the goads" (Acts 26:14), in vain; it hurt him to do so. He "suffered the loss of all things" (Phil. 3:8) for the sake of the Crucified, though he learned to count that loss an incomparable gain (Phil 3:9). When the Lord appeared to Saul and turned the persecutor of the church into the preacher of "the faith he once tried to destroy" (Gal. 1:23), the church "had peace" (Acts 9:31). But Herod Agrippa II, A.D. 44, "laid violent hands on some who belonged to the church . . . killed James the brother of John with the sword," and had Peter in prison ready to be brought out to the people who were pleased by the execution of James (Acts 12:1-5). But the Lord sent His angel and rescued Peter "from the hand of Herod and from all that the Jewish people were expecting" (Acts 12:11) and sent him "to another place" (Acts 12:17). The Lord set him free to plead the cause of Gentile freedom from the Law in faith (Acts 15:6-11), to strengthen his brethren (cf. Luke 22:32) among the Gentiles (1 Peter), and to glorify God by means of a death meekly endured after the manner of his crucified Lord (cf. John 21:19). The Lord smote down the persecuting king in mid-career (Acts 12:20-23), while the defenseless "word of God grew and multiplied." (Acts 12:24)

When Paul "boasts" of all that marks him as a servant of Christ, he speaks of himself as a servant of the Crucified, "with far greater labors, far more imprisonments, with countless beatings, and often near death" (2 Cor. 11:23). He speaks of sufferings at the hands of Jews, of "the forty lashes less one" which Judaic interpretation of the Law allowed (Deut. 25:3) and of stoning (2 Cor. 11:24-25); he speaks also of suffering at the hands of Roman officials ("beaten with rods," 2 Cor. 11:25; cf. Acts 16:22). And he enumerates among the dangers which constantly threatened him on his journeyings "danger from my own people, danger from Gentiles" (2 Cor. 11:26). As the Roman Pilate and the Jewish Sanhedrin joined in inflicting the cross upon the Crucified, so the Roman world and Jewry joined in their attack upon those who proclaimed the good news of the Crucified. In the Gentile world, too, the glory of the church was glory *sub cruce tecta,* hidden under the cross.

True, Gentile officials more than once intervened to shield the messengers of the Crucified from popular hostility or Judaic malice, or both in combination (cf., e.g., Acts 18:12-16; 19:30-41; 21:27-36), and Paul could appeal to the Roman emperor in order to obtain from his court the fair decision which it seemed impossible to obtain in the heated atmosphere of his Jewish homeland (Acts 25:9-12). But on the other hand it is to be remembered that Paul speaks of being beaten no less than three times by Roman rods (only one instance is recorded in Acts); and there is little reason to suppose that the Christian witness in word and action was ever popular anywhere in the Roman world. The "danger from Gentiles" was no doubt a danger to Paul's converts as well as to Paul, but in earlier years it was probably more often danger from popular hostility (issuing in slanderous accusations and pogromlike action) toward an odd group of nonconforming and therefore suspicious characters than from any official persecution of the church. That is the picture we get of the position of the church from 1 Peter (1 Peter 3:16-17; 4:4, 13-14, 16; cf. 2:13-17). The "fiery ordeal" (1 Peter 4:12) and the "suffering . . . of the brotherhood throughout the world" (1 Peter 5:9) were probably due more to popular suspicion than to any official governmental action.

But the strange "otherness" of Christians (cf. 1 Peter 4:4) gave them the reputation of being animated by a "hatred for the human race" (as a Roman historian later called it). It was this that brought upon the Christians in the city of Rome the first official Gentile persecution. When large portions of the poorer quarters of Rome were destroyed by fire A.D. 64, it was popularly supposed that the emperor Nero had himself set the fire in order to clear ground for one of his ambitious building projects. When all other means failed, Nero sought to divert suspicion and hatred from himself by fixing the blame for the disastrous fire on the already-unpopular Christians and put large numbers of them to death with such cruel and ostentatious savagery that it roused a revulsion of popular feeling. The persecution was confined to Rome and was short-lived; but it brought home to the church hidden under the cross how precarious her position in the Empire was, how the kingdom of God and His Anointed is perpetually liable to attack by Satan and his Antichrist, and it fixed Nero in Christian memory as a classic example of the antichristian beast; many touches in the picture of the beast in The Revelation to John are allusive references to Emperor Nero (see the commentary).

The church has been described as "an anvil that hath worn out many hammers." There were many hammerblows in the first century, and they struck notable sparks of inspired witness to the church's durability (cf. Rom. 8:17, 31-39). The hammerblow which struck from the anvil of the church the spark of inspired witness called The Revelation to John fell on the church most probably about A.D. 95 (some scholars date the book in the time of Nero), and it fell in the Roman province of Asia (in western Asia Minor).

There, in Ephesus, the Gospel of the Crucified had collided, as early as the 50s of the first century, with the peculiarly fervid Asiatic pagan religious zeal, no less fervid and more violent because it was coupled with a commercial self-interest (Acts 19:21-41). The enraged shout raised by Demetrius and his fellow craftsmen, "Great is Artemis of the Ephesians" (Acts 19:28), was not merely or wholly the cry of confused and ignorant trade-unionist zeal for the prestige and profit of their trade. There was probably at least an admixture of concern for the "magnificence" of Artemis, whom "all Asia and the world" worshiped (Acts 19:27). There, in Ephesus, neither Judaic blasphemy (Acts 19:9-10) nor the competitive greed of magic (Acts 19:11-19) could stay the progress of the Gospel. "All the residents of Asia heard the word of the Lord . . . . The word of the Lord grew and prevailed mightily" (Acts 19:10, 20). What Paul planted in Asia, others watered, notably John the son of Zebedee in his latter ministry. The province of Asia became the most thoroughly Christian region in the Roman Empire.

Where God sows wheat, the enemy sows weeds (Matt. 13:24-30). In Asia the religious cult of the Roman emperor had early been warmly welcomed and was assiduously cultivated, city vying with city to express its devotion to the deified emperor. When the emperor Domitian (81—96 A.D.) went beyond his predecessors in asserting his claim to divinity, calling himself "Lord and God," he no doubt found in the province of Asia willing worshipers and propagandists enough. As The Revelation to John expresses it: The antichristian beast rising from the sea (i. e., coming from Rome, cf. comments on 13:1) found in the beast rising from the earth (i. e., in the province of Asia, cf. comments on 13:11) an antichristian prophet to play the role of anti-Spirit to his Antichrist (cf. 13:11-18), to assert the Antichrist's authority and to build up the religious power and fascination of his antichurch ("Babylon," cf. Chs. 17—18).

Thus the church in Asia was confronted by the claim of the kingdom of God and the counterclaim of the kingdom of Satan. Since the counterclaim of the kingdom of Satan was expressed in ways that permeated social and civic life (see the letters to Pergamum and to Thyatira, 2:12-29), claim and counterclaim presented themselves in a concrete and not-to-be-evaded way. The pressure upon the church was intensified by the enmity of the "synagogue of Satan," as John calls the hostile Jews (2:9; 3:9). The church was therefore understandably more conscious of her "tribulation" in Jesus than she was of the glory of the Kingdom and of the necessity of the "patient endurance" of hope under tribulation. (Cf. 1:9.)

The letters to the seven churches (Chs. 2—3) make it clear that the church in Asia was not an ideal church, superhumanly perfect. The activity and influence of the Nicolaitans at Ephesus and Pergamum and the not-unsuccessful pretensions of the prophetess "Jezebel" at Thyatira (2:6, 15, 20) were fulfillments of Jesus' prophecy that in times of tribulation (Matt. 24:9) "false prophets will arise and lead many astray" (Matt. 24:11). And at Ephesus, at least, His prophecy that "love will grow cold" (Matt. 24:12) was being proved true (Rev. 2:4). In the declension of the church's love there lay the danger of compromise and apostasy, and the suasion of the Balaamlike Nicolaitans and of the Jezebellike prophetess of Thyatira heightened the danger.

17

The church in Asia needed a genuinely prophetic word to steady, sustain, and inspirit her in the danger which threatened her from without and within. In the person of John God raised up for her a prophet, a genuine prophet from her own midst (cf. Deut. 18:18), one who shared with the church in Jesus "the tribulation and kingdom and the patient endurance" (1:9), himself relegated by the Roman authorities to the island of Patmos "on account of the word of God and the testimony of Jesus" (1:9). He was empowered by his Lord (1:1-2) to speak the needed prophetic word which could keep the eyes of the church fixed on the promised kingdom in the midst of threatening tribulation and could keep alive and buoyant her hope, in patient endurance. The prophetic word that was needed to make all who hear and keep it blessed (1:3) was the basic New Testament word, "the word of the cross" (1 Cor. 1:18), the proclamation of "Christ and him crucified" (1 Cor. 2:2). John proclaimed the Gospel of the Crucified in both its indicative and its imperative form. His prophetic word is both the song of the triumph of the Crucified and the continuation of Jesus' call of "Follow me."

John, moved by the same Spirit that taught Paul (1 Cor. 2:12-13), is determined to know nothing in the church except "Christ and him crucified" (1 Cor. 2:2). At the very beginning of his words of prophecy, in his epistolary greeting, he invokes upon his hearers grace and peace from Jesus Christ, the faithful Witness whose unshrinking "testimony before Pontius Pilate" (1 Tim. 6:13; cf. John 18:37) took Him into death upon the cross and beyond death into a life wherein He is "the ruler of kings on earth" (Rev. 1:5). The first doxology of John's doxological book is a doxology to the Crucified, "to him who loves us and has freed us from our sins by his blood" (1:5-6). It is the Crucified, the One "pierced" by men, who is proclaimed as returning in a glory which shall make all the tribes of the earth wail in remorse for having pierced Him (1:7). The flaming glory of the Son of Man in John's inaugural vision, that Figure clad in a robe and girt with a girdle woven from golden threads from the Old Testament (1:12-16), culminates in the glory of the Crucified, who lays His compassionate hand on His dumbfounded prophet and says, "Fear not, I am . . . the living one; I died, and behold I

18

am alive for evermore, and I have the keys of Death and Hades" (1:17-18). It is this Crucified One who commissions the prophet: "now [or "therefore"] write." (1:19)

The characteristic title of Christ in The Revelation to John is "the Lamb," sometimes specifically characterized as a sacrificial lamb by the mention of "blood" or by the modifier "slain." The term occurs 28 times in the book. The ultimate background, besides the general reference to sacrifice, is Is. 53:7, where the servant of the Lord goes meekly into His atoning suffering and death "like a lamb that is led to the slaughter" (cf. Acts 8:32-35). John the Baptist's acclamation of Jesus as "the Lamb of God, who takes away the sin of the world" (John 1:29) was no doubt intended to recall the lamb of Is. 53; and Paul's reference to Christ as "our paschal lamb" (1 Cor. 5:7) suggests that we are to think also of the Passover lamb whose blood delivered Israel on the night when the firstborn of Egypt were slain. (Ex. 12:21-27)

The Lamb bears the mark of slaughter, the sign of the sacrificial victim (Rev. 5:6, 9, 12; 13:8) whose blood expiates the sins of the world. To Him "the four living creatures and the twenty-four elders" around God's throne sing:

Thou wast slain and by thy blood
didst ransom men for God (5:9).

The servants of God wear the white garments of purity and victory by virtue of the blood of the Lamb. (7:14)

In undergoing death the Lamb has conquered death. He lives for evermore as the archetypal Conqueror, bearing the insignia of omnipotence and omniscience ("seven horns" and "seven eyes," 5:6), in token that He has authority over His conquered enemies, "Death and Hades" (1:18). Thus as One who has conquered and sat down on His Father's throne (3:21), He is Lord of the future. He can open the sealed scroll of God's counsels, release the steeds of God who carry out God's purpose in the world (Chs. 5—6), and be forever the Good Shepherd who guides His people to "springs of living water" (7:17). He stands on Mount Zion already triumphant, surrounded by the 144,000 who bear His redeeming name and are already celebrating His final victory (14:1, 3). His victory is sure; though the forces of Antichrist "make war on the Lamb . . . the Lamb will conquer them, for he is Lord of lords and King of kings." (17:14)

As the blood of the Lamb has ransomed men for God (5:9), His "wrath" will judge all who hold cheap and refuse that ransoming (6:16-17). Being inscribed in the Lamb's book of life, that alone will protect a man from the attack of Antichrist in the world (13:8) and will deliver him from the torment of the lake of fire in the judgment to come. (20:15)

In the world to come the Lamb shall reign supreme; "the throne of God and of the Lamb" shall be one throne (22:3). As God is the light of His new world, the Lamb is its lamp (21:23). He is one with the Lord God the Almighty also in that He is in person the temple of the new city of God (21:22; cf. John 2:19-22). In Him man may draw near to God and behold His face. To be always with the Lord (1 Thess. 4:17), that is the desire and the prayer of His people (Rev. 22:17); and God's answer to that prayer is the Lamb. The church is the bride of the Lamb and shall become His wife (21:9); the high festal joy of that final union is signalized by the decking-out of the bride "with fine linen, bright and pure . . . the righteous deeds of the saints" (19:7-8) and by the holy merriment of "the marriage supper of the Lamb." (19:9)

The goal and crown of the life of the church, the bride of the Lamb, is that she be forever united with Him. It is therefore natural and inevitable that until she reaches that goal and until that crown is achieved her life should be a *following* Him (cf. Jer. 2:2), "following" in the sense in which Jesus used the word, a sense nowhere else in the New Testament echoed so completely as in John's words of prophecy. At two high points in his book the word "follow" occurs in the pregnant sense impressed upon it by Jesus. In 14:4 those who stand on Mount Zion with the Lamb and with their new song anticipate His triumph over all the force and fascination of the Antichrist and the anti-Spirit (cf. Chs. 12— 13), those devoted virgin souls "redeemed from mankind as first fruits for God and the Lamb" who speak the truth and die rather than assent to the satanic lie (14:5), those martyrs are described as men "who *follow* the Lamb wherever he goes." In 19:14, when the true Rider on the white horse of victory has appeared (cf. 6:2 for the pseudo-Christian caricature of the Rider on the white horse), "the armies of heaven" clad in garments of victory *follow* in the train of Him who "is called Faithful and True" (19:11) and "The Word of God" (19:13), who is destined to judge and make war in righteousness (19:11) and to destroy His enemies and all their host (19:19-21). Those who follow are those who follow Him into defeat and death (cf. Matt. 16:24); trusting the promise of Him who is called Faithful and True, they find victory and life: "Whoever loses his life for my sake will find it." (Matt. 16:25)

They find victory and life; they are the conquerors, followers of the archetypal Conqueror who "has conquered, so that he can open the scroll" which contains the counsels of God which determine the history of the world and mankind (Rev. 5:5). The Lamb has conquered and will conquer (17:14). The victory belongs to Him who "in righteousness ... judges and makes war" (19:11). Whatever the appearances to the contrary, He is the Conqueror, and He alone. The anti-Christian rider on the white horse who heads the procession of God's destructive agents let loose (by the Lamb! 6:1) upon the world may appear to be invincible as he goes out "conquering and to conquer" (6:2), but the victory belongs to the Lamb whose day of wrath shall bring all men low in terror (6:17). The beast that ascends from the bottomless pit may "conquer" the witnesses of God whose testimony is "a torment to those who dwell on the earth" (11:10); but though the witnesses lie killed and degraded in the city "where their Lord was crucified" (11:8), they go through dishonor and death to life and victory, as their Lord went before them (11:11-13). Though the beast who rises from the sea may conquer the saints of God, he can "conquer" only because he is "*allowed* to make war on the saints and to conquer them" (13:7), allowed by God, who thus tests, tempers, and makes victorious the faith of His saints. "This is the victory that overcomes the world, our faith." (1 John 5:4)

In faith the saints conquer; that is, they enter into the victory won for them by the Lamb that was slain. Him they "follow" into death and into victory. In faith they have conquered the accuser, Satan, because they hold firm in One whom the accuser cannot accuse, One who testified to the

21

truth of God with His death (Rev. 12:11). In His love He included all men in Himself and made all men innocent (cf. 1:5). In His love for man He expressed His love for God (cf. Matt. 22:34-40) and did God's will. Because God has chosen the saints and inscribed them "in the Lamb's book of life" (21:27), they can be His faithful ones (17:14), who emerge victorious from their conflict with the beast; their victory is the Lamb's victory, and the victor-song they sing is "the song of the Lamb." (15:3)

To the followers of the Lamb, to those persecuted conquerors who believe, in hope against hope, in the Victor Lamb—to them the great promises of The Revelation to John are spoken. The conqueror shall "eat of the tree of life" in paradise regained (2:7); no "second death" can deprive the conqueror of the life he has gained by dying as a follower of the Lamb (2:10-11). The conqueror shall feed on the hidden manna, "the bread of God ... which comes down from heaven and gives life to the world" (John 6:33; Rev. 2:17). The conqueror who follows Christ and keeps Christ's works to the end (2:26) shall participate in Christ's rule over the nations. Him Christ will confess before His Father; his name shall be ineradicably inscribed in the book of life, and the white garments of victory and heavenly festivity shall clothe him for evermore (3:5). Bearing the name of God, the name of God's new Jerusalem, and Christ's own new name, the conqueror shall stand immovable as a pillar in the temple of God (3:12). The conqueror shall share the enthronement with God which *the* Conqueror has received and holds. "He who conquers shall have this heritage" (21:7), all the blessings of God's consummated creation under a new heaven on a new earth, all the blessing of God's consummated will to communion with man in the new Jerusalem.

One might go on to draw the line from Jesus' beatitude upon those persecuted for His sake (Matt. 5:10-12) to the beatitude pronounced in The Revelation to John on those "who die in the Lord henceforth" (14:13)—"henceforth," now that the onset of the anti-Trinity bodes persecution and death for all "who follow the Lamb wherever he goes" (14:4). But perhaps enough has been said to show that as surely as the indicative Gospel of The Revelation to John is the Gospel of Christ and Him crucified, so the imperative Gospel of this book is the ultimate reverberation of Jesus' "Follow me!"

B. Luther's Formal Objection: The Style of The Revelation to John

In view of the evidence of The Revelation to John itself, it is difficult to be sympathetic with Luther's substantive objection that in it "Christ is neither taught nor recognized." It is easier to sympathize with his formal objection, that the style of the book is cryptic, lacking in the forthright simplicity and literal directness of a genuine apostolic and prophetic witness to Christ.

On first encounter the world of The Revelation to John does seem to be a wild and mysterious world. What are we to make of this strange land, where a slain lamb with unimaginable seven horns and seven eyes is conqueror and in the power of a counqueror takes a sealed scroll from the hand of God and unseals it? What are we to make of a land where the unsealing of a scroll does not merely make accessible information hitherto unknown and unknowable but releases horsemen mounted on white, red, black, and pale horses who course across the world creating havoc as they go? What shall we make of a lamb who suddenly appears as a shepherd, who has a bride and a marriage supper, of a lamb who shares a throne with God, who is the lamp and the temple of a new Jerusalem? What shall we make of angel trumpeters whose trumpet blasts bring plagues on land and sea, on rivers and fountains, and on sun, moon, and stars? Of trumpets whose sound evokes a weird plague of locusts from the bottomless pit, locusts whose sting is scorpionlike, whose king is the Destroyer? What shall we make of trumpets that call forth those troops of cavalry from beyond the Euphrates whose number is as unimaginable as their appearance is uncanny and their attack dreadful? One need but mention the appearance of an angel from heaven who is wrapped in a cloud, has a rainbow over his head, a face like the sun, and legs like pillars of fire, who raises his hand in solemn oath and calls out in a voice that causes the seven thunders to sound, thunders whose message the prophet is forbidden to record. What does it mean that this angel has a little scroll open in his hand, that the prophet is bidden to take the scroll and eat it, that he finds this indigestible morsel sweet in the mouth and bitter in the stomach?

We are accustomed, from our reading of the Bible, to bold and picturesque language, to poetry that stretches the imagination to follow and taxes the mind to understand. But we are hardly prepared for this mass of heaped-up and extravagant imagery, presented merely as imagery and, except for two instances (7:13-17; 17:6-18), presented without explanatory comment. Part of our difficulty may be due to our "modern" unwillingness or inability to submit to the discipline required of the reader in apprehending high poetry, our laziness in the use of imaginative reason, and our consequent distrust of poetry as a vehicle of serious thought. Yet the reason lies deeper than that; we seem to have lost (or at least our conscious minds have lost, whatever we may have instinctively retained) the universally human understanding and appreciation of the *symbol*.

What is a symbol? A symbol is the shortest of shorthands. Whether it be expressed in language, in two-dimensional drawing and painting, or in three-dimensional form, a symbol expresses little but suggests much. It expresses little, that is, for the uninitiated, the outsider. It illustrates in an extreme form Luther's dictum that "unless a man knows what is being talked about, he cannot make sense of what is being said." A symbol is language of an "insider" for "insiders." Take the symbol of the cross, in its simplest form merely a vertical line transversed by a horizontal line. How much this simple symbol suggests when used by an insider for insiders may be illustrated by Alford's use of the sign of the cross in his baptismal hymn:

> In token that thou shalt not fear
> Christ crucified to own,
> We print the cross upon thee here
> And stamp thee his alone.

> In token that thou shalt not flinch
> Christ's combat to maintain,
> But 'neath his banner manfully
> Firm at thy post remain:

24

In token that thou too shalt tread
The path he traveled by,
Endure the cross, despise the shame;
And sit thee down on high:

Thus outwardly and visibly
We seal thee for his own;
And may the brow that wears his cross
Hereafter share his crown.

No insider would complain that Alford, when he wrote the hymn for the baptism of his own child, was overinterpreting the symbol of the cross; it does suggest and evoke what the hymn says. But an "outsider," unacquainted with the Gospel of Christ and Him crucified, might well be puzzled or even scornful at seeing all that Alford "reads into" the simple ceremonial of intersecting vertical and horizontal lines drawn in the air over an infant's head.

A symbol is communication by an insider to insiders; the force of a symbol can therefore be sensed and appreciated only by an insider. (It is better to say "sensed" than "understood," since it is the peculiar virtue of a symbol that its force can be felt and its power appreciated even when it is but dimly understood.)

The symbols of The Revelation to John are not a form of hocus-pocus, intended to conceal; as John's own title to the book indicates, its intention is to reveal. The symbols have the effect of concealing only for those unwilling to come "inside" and thus get eyes to see the invisible. And one gets "inside" not by cultivating cleverness in guessing at possibilities or probabilities and not by undisciplined and uncontrolled use of the imagination (important as imagination is for the apprehension of symbols) but by going through doors provided by the book itself, by following the clues given by The Revelation to John itself.

The first and most important of the doors which lead "inside," into the suggestive and evocative domain of the symbol, is the Gospel of Christ and Him crucified (see Part A of this Introduction). John's opening ascription of praise "to him who loves us and has freed us from our sins by his blood and made us a kingdom, priests to his God and Father, to him be glory and dominion for ever and ever" (1:5-6) gives us, in forthright language, the clue to the symbol of the Lamb that is both sacrificial Victim and the Victor, possessed of a dominion and glory which are wholly unlamblike and nothing short of divine. *This* Lamb can have a bride and, once "inside," we have no difficulty in apprehending that this Lamb has 12 apostles whose names grace the foundations of the walls of God's new Jerusalem and mark the city as the workmanship and the gift of God.

The second door which leads "inside" is the Old Testament. No one else among the authors of the books of the New Testament has taken so seriously as John and has followed so completely Jesus' word: "The scriptures [that is, the Old Testament] . . . it is they that bear witness to me" (John 5:39). John draws on (though he never formally introduces the Old Testament word with an "It is written") all parts of the Old Testament, the Law, the former and the latter Prophets, and the Writings. His "favorites" seem to be the Psalms, Isaiah, Ezekiel, Daniel—and Daniel is the favorite among the favorites. His first indication of the content of the revelation given to him by Jesus Christ, "what must soon take place" (1:1), is a phrase from Daniel (Dan. 2:28), and the designation of Christ and Antichrist as "Son of man" and as "beast" respectively have as their background the vision of Dan. 7.

But the whole Old Testament is laid under contribution; a whole battery of symbols is illumined and made meaningful by reference to all parts of the Old Testament. One may choose examples almost at random: The rainbow round the throne of the Lord God Almighty or over the head of the mighty angel who holds the little scroll, the effectual trumpets that do the work of God, the exodus of the servants of God celebrated in "the song of Moses . . . and the song of the Lamb" (15:3), varicolored horses as executors of God's purposes, the prophet devouring a scroll as a symbol of his inspiration, the harlot Babylon as the oppressive enemy of the people of God—all these are Old Testament language.

Indeed, it is difficult to formulate John's indebtedness to the Old Testament, so rich and so all-pervasive is the language and thought of the Old Testament. John, as it were, thinks and speaks Old Testament throughout, from the echo of Daniel in 1:1 to the echo of Genesis in 22:19. The last book of our Bible puts its witness into the perspective of the whole Biblical witness and summons the whole company of God's witnesses to be witnesses to Christ and Him crucified. The Lutheran Confessions might summon John as their crown witness when they pledge themselves to the "writings of the Old and New Testament as the pure and clear fountain of Israel," from which Israel may drink and live.

"I am a part of all that I have met." When the Holy Spirit takes and uses a man, He does not unman him; He does not strip him of his past and his accumulated memories. An inspired man is, as every man is, "a part of all that he has met." A third door to the "inside" of The Revelation to John and an "inside" apprehension of his symbols is, therefore, the possession of some knowledge of what John has met as a first-century Jewish man living in the Roman Empire.

As a citizen in the Roman Empire, John would know Rome as the city of seven hills (17:9). He would know something of the Roman emperors and their history, especially the history of Nero, the first great persecutor of the church, and of Domitian, the current emperor (A.D. 95), who styled himself "Lord and God" and accepted the worship of the Roman provinces, where men outdid one another in their devotion to the deified emperor. He would know what mysterious terror the region beyond the Euphrates held for Roman minds, how Romans trembled at the thought of the Parthian mounted archers, terrible alike in attack and in retreat (cf. comments on 9:14, 19). John would know what significance was popularly attached to the seven stars as a symbol of worldwide dominion (1:16, 20). Above all, he would know at first hand the brute power and the fearful fascination of the beast rising from the sea. (Ch. 13)

As the man of Jewish descent, language, and culture that he obviously was, John was acquainted with and influenced by a form of Judaic religious literature which modern scholars have classified as "apocalyptic." Apocalyptic literature elaborated certain elements or aspects of Old Testament prophecy, found in such passages and books as Is. 24—27, Zech. 9—14, Ezekiel, Joel, and Daniel. It sought to interpret all history on the basis of purported visionary experiences of the author. It was especially interested in eschatology, that is, in the end of history and the ushering in of the world to come. It utilized pictures, allegories, and symbols (which soon became traditional); numbers, colors, and stars were in these images endowed with a profound significance. Books of this type were The Book of Enoch, The Book of Jubilees, Fourth Esdras, The Assumption of Moses.

Formally, The Revelation to John belongs to this class; apocalyptic furnished the familiar vocabulary of its speech. The influence of apocalyptic on The Revelation to John can be and often has been exaggerated. The Revelation to John is set apart from the general run of apocalyptic literature by profound differences. Apocalyptic itself drew heavily on the Old Testament; John draws even more heavily. In fact, it is the Old Testament itself and not apocalyptic that constitutes the immediate background and the richest source for Revelation. Revelation is at bottom much more deeply akin to the Old Testament than it is to the apocalyptic which it resembles so strongly on the formal side. Other differences are equally striking. Apocalyptic works are generally pseudonymous; that is, they claim some great figure from Israel's past, such as Enoch, as author; and the past course of history as known to the actual author is made a prediction in the mouth of the purported author. John, however, writes in his own name. Apocalyptic has speculative interests and seeks to calculate the times and seasons of the world's days and the world's end. John has no such speculative interest; he does not aim to satisfy men's curiosity but to give them hope and courage, and he does not attempt to calculate the approach of the end. "I come quickly" is the burden of the revelation of Christ as given to John. The visions of apocalyptic betray their origin; they are the fantasies of men. The visions of John have on them the stamp of genuine visionary experience; they are not products of the study. If apocalyptic may be termed literary meditation on prophetic themes, Revelation is genuine prophecy, a prophecy which uses apocalyptic motifs and forms insofar, and only insofar, as they are legitimate explications of Old Testament prophetic themes and are germane to its own thoroughly Christ-centered proclamation.

The Revelation to John is written in the language of symbol, by an insider for insiders. But the "insideness" is not an insoluble mystery; there are doors that open inward for those who will take the trouble to use them, clues to guide one inward if one will take the trouble to follow them. And thousands upon thousands who have lived bravely and died well in the strength afforded them by this book will testify that the reward is worth the trouble. It is a letter from the disciple whom Jesus loved to the church in a time when the church is most churchly, when every hope but the one real Hope has been taken from her, when prayer is not a last resort but the only resort. The apparent weakness of The Revelation to John is its real strength. This strange language has power to keep the church the praying church:

> O where are kings and empires now
> Of old that went and came?
> But, Lord, Thy church is praying yet,
> A thousand years the same.

The prayer that it empowers and teaches us to pray is as simple as the promise which prompts it is great, the promise and the prayer with which the book closes:

> Surely I am coming soon . . . .
> Come, Lord Jesus! (22:20)

INTRODUCTION
1:1-8

Opening Statement with Blessing
1:1-3

1 For the church, wind-swept and storm-tossed on the waves of a history in which evil and Satanic powers are, apparently, the powers which prevail, there is only one voice that can speak assuring and empowering comfort: the voice of her Lord (cf. Matt. 8:23-27). The title given by John to his book in these first verses indicates that The Revelation to John is that voice. The revelation given in vision and word is the revelation of Jesus Christ; it has been given Him by God. Jesus Christ both receives from His Father and gives to men the revelation which only God can give (cf. Matt. 11:25-27; John 3:34-35; 5:20-23; 8:28; 12:48-50; 17:8), insight into the mystery of "what must soon take place." This phrase echoes the language of the Old Testament (Dan. 2:28-29, 45) and recalls the substance of the prophet Daniel too, the conflict between the seemingly superior kingdoms of this world, demonically motivated, and the unpromising kingdom of God which is nevertheless destined to conquer and prevail at the end of days. The Revelation to John will tell and interpret the history of the conflict between the kingdom of God and the kingdom of Satan. The revelation can give strength to His servants, so that they will be able, in the power of His promises, to hope, endure, and conquer in uncompromising loyalty to Him (cf. 2:10) amid threatening persecution (cf. 1:9). Jesus Christ sends His angel as the Lord sent His messengers of old, and He makes John, His servant-prophet, the vehicle of His word to men, just as the Lord of old revealed "His secret to His servants the prophets." (Amos 3:7)

2 The word of the prophet John is therefore, like the word of the ancient prophets, "the word of God," the declaration of God's purpose, powerful and inviolable (cf.

22:18-19); it is the "testimony of Jesus Christ," who is in person the very Word of God (cf. 19:13; John 1:1), by whom God has declared His will. "All that he [John] saw" has on it the impress of a first-century man who knows and loves as his Lord the Jesus we know from the gospels, a man saturated with the language and the substance of the Old Testament and acquainted with the conventions of "apocalyptic" literature (cf. Introduction pp. 27—29). But what John saw is no product of his imagination nor an essence distilled from his intuitions. John does not originate revelation; he only *witnesses,* but he witnesses to what is nothing less than the word of God.

3 This word of God will bless, so the first of Revelation's seven beatitudes declares (cf. 14:13; 16:15; 19:9; 20:6; 22:7; 22:14), all those whom it touches. It will bless the lector who reads John's prophetic word in the assemblies of the worshiping churches (cf. 1:11), and it will bless all those who hear the word from his lips and keep it, that is, receive it from him "as what it really is, the word of God which is at work in . . . believers" (1 Thess. 2:13). "Believers"—the word of God asks for faith; it is a word to be kept and held fast "in an honest and good heart," so that the hearer, like good soil, "brings forth fruit in patience" (Luke 8:15). "The time is near." There is no time now to luxuriate in the hope of the coming feast, as the five foolish maidens in Jesus' parable did (Matt. 25:1-13). It is time to heed and keep the word of Him who says (in the letter to the church in Philadelphia, 3:11): "I am coming soon; hold fast ["hold fast" reproduces the same Greek word which is here, in 1:3, rendered "keep"] what you have, so that no one may seize your crown." What the church has now, amid the "tribulation" of impending persecution (1:9), is the word of her Lord, and the church can look to receive more only by really having what she has; otherwise even what she has will be taken from her. (Matt. 13:12)

The Epistolary Greeting, with Doxology
1:4-6

4 The practical character of this prophetic word (cf. 3), its urgent this-means-you character, is underscored by the

fact that the book as a whole has the form of a letter. The features of an apostolic letter, familiar to us from the letters of Paul, are all here: the name of the sender (who calls himself plainly and simply "John"; he does not clothe himself in the raiment of some memorable figure of the past such as Enoch or Baruch, as the authors of Judaic apocalyptic writings do, cf. Introduction, p.); the name of the recipients (the seven churches of the Roman province of Asia, cf. 11 and Chs. 2 and 3); the familiar greeting of "grace" and "peace" (the unearned active favor of God and the whole and sound well-being which the gracious lifting-up of His shining countenance in Christ creates, cf. Num. 6:26; 2 Cor. 4:6); the opening thanksgiving, or doxology, 5b-6 (cf. Rom. 1:8; 1 Cor. 1:4-9; 2 Cor. 1:3-7). And the book closes, as it begins, with a common epistolary feature: the invocation of the grace of the Lord Jesus upon the readers, 22:21 (cf. Rom. 16:20; 1 Cor. 16:23; 2 Cor. 13:14; Gal. 6:18). The Author of this grace and peace is solemnly identified as God the enthroned King ("throne") who once revealed Himself to Moses as the God who was, graciously and powerfully, with Abraham, Isaac, and Jacob and made of these "wandering Arameans . . . a nation, great, mighty, and populous" (Deut. 26:5), and declared His will to visit and redeem His people in the name "I AM" (Ex. 3:14; cf. 15-20): His "being" is a graciously active being, the being of the God-at-hand. He who "was" and "is" is Lord of the future too; He is "to come." He sits enthroned over all the future of men, and in His hand is the book wherein the destinies of men are written. He knows those who are His own (Chs. 4 and 5; cf. 2 Tim. 2:19), and the prospect of their imperiled future need hold no endless terrors for them.

His is the Spirit, mightier than the history-making men and horses of Egypt and wiser than those who trust in horses and horsemen (Is. 31:1-3). The Spirit will be present in all His plenitude ("seven spirits") among the seven troubled churches; His wise and healing word will be spoken to them in "the words of prophecy" (v. 3) of this book and will make them capable of victory with the victorious Word of God. (2:7, 11, 17, 26-29; 3:5-6, 12-13, 21-22; cf. 19:11-16)

5 His is the Anointed King, the Christ, great David's greater Son, concerning whom prophet (Is. 55:3-5) and psalmist (Ps. 89:27, 36-37) had spoken such great promises; in the power of God's "everlasting covenant" (Is. 55:3; cf. 2 Sam. 23:5) He was to outtop even David as "witness to the peoples" (Is. 55:4), that is, as a witness to the presence and power of the Lord's steadfast love. The promise that the Lord would not lie to David (Ps. 89:35) but would establish his descendants forever (Ps. 89:4) came overwhelmingly true; Jesus, "descended from David according to the flesh" (Rom. 1:3), proved to be a "witness," "firstborn," and "highest of the kings of the earth" (Ps. 89:27) in a dimension which dwarfed all David's greatness. He went into death as faithful witness for the truth of God (John 18:37) and so conquered death. He rose from the dead to become "the firstborn among many brethren" (Rom. 8:29) who are predestined to be conformed to the image of the Son who "will never die again" (Rom. 6:9) but will live and reign forever not merely as "highest" (Ps. 89:27) but as "the ruler of kings on earth." No kings on earth nor any death that kings devise can separate the church from the grace and peace of God in Christ. (Cf. Rom. 8:39)

5b-6 Jesus promised His disciples that He would build His church, victorious over death, and in the same breath, as it were, foretold His own redeeming passion and death (Matt. 16:18, 21). In one breath the prophet likewise ascribes to Him the glory that is His as the One whose love moved Him to shed His blood in order to provide the "plenteous redemption" wherewith (so said the ancient promise, Ps. 130:7-8) the Lord would "redeem Israel from all his iniquities"; and in the same breath he ascribes to Him the dominion which is His by virtue of His payment of the ransom (cf. Matt. 20:28) which "freed us from our sins." Now the Accuser can bring accusation against men before God no more (12:10), and now Satan's warfare against the angels and the people of God is in vain (12:7-9, 13-17), now the Christ can build His church and can do what the Law could not do, make of His people the free, living company of kings and priests who embody God's reign and mediate His presence on earth. (Rom. 8:2-4; Ex. 19:6)

Introit: The Promise Concerning the Return of the Crucified and God's Self-Attestation as the Alpha and Omega
1:7-8

7 The doxology to Christ (5b-6) provides a transition to two versicles of a liturgical character, a sort of introit to the worship service of which the reading of the letter was to be a part. The first of the two versicles speaks of the return of Christ in words derived from Dan. 7:13 and Zech. 12:10: The Son of Man of Dan. 7:13, once rejected and crucified ("pierced," Zech. 12:10), will return in the glory in which Daniel beheld Him, "with the clouds"; and as His manifested divine splendor and the true significance of His suffering burst upon men, they will be moved to a universal wailing of remorse. The glory of His "dominion" (Dan. 7:14) will then be as manifest as the glory of the Redeemer is hidden now; for the faith of the prophet there can be no doubt of that ("Even so. Amen.")—our Lord had spoken of His return in glory in language likewise derived from Daniel and Zechariah. (Matt. 24:30)

8 In the second versicle the Lord God Himself speaks. He reveals Himself as the Lord who once revealed Himself to Moses at the burning bush in order to deliver His people from their bondage in Egypt, as the Lord God of the covenant who is the living Center of His people's history as He has been its Beginning and shall be its End; for He is Alpha and Omega, the first and last letters of the Greek alphabet. He is the living Lord of Hosts ("the Almighty") who presses irresistibly on toward His own and His people's victorious future. (Cf. 21:6)

These two verses are the *cantus firmus* on which all the music of The Revelation to John is based. That music, for all its unshrinking realism in facing the facts of human sin and of satanic revolt, is therefore a song of triumph, one great visionary development of Jesus' word: "Blessed are those who are persecuted for righteousness' sake, for theirs is the kingdom of heaven." (Matt. 5:10)

The First Three Visions:
The Church of Christ
and the Powers of This World
1:9—11:19

The Inaugural Vision: The Seven Letters
1:9—3:22

The Prophet's Inaugural Vision:
Christ in the Midst of His Church
1:9-20

9 The prophet is one with the churches to whom he speaks the word of God; he is their brother and partner (as men who have their life and future in Jesus, the crucified and risen Lord, 18). In this age and on this earth the kingdom which Jesus proclaimed and inaugurated means tribulation for those whom Christ had made kings, and calls for patient endurance (Matt. 10:34-39; Acts 14:22). The prophet, as he shares in his people's privilege, shares in their "tribulation" too: That tribulation is now the threat of persecution. The persecuting arm of Rome, whose shadow has fallen over the church, has reached the proclaimer of "the word of God and the testimony of Jesus" (cf. 1:2); he has been relegated to Patmos, a little island (10x6 miles) off the coast of Asia Minor, not far from Miletus, one of the islands much used by the Roman emperors as a place of banishment for disturbers of the Roman peace.

10 There he was privileged to behold a vision, as the prophets Isaiah, Jeremiah, and Ezekiel had been before him (Is. 6; Jer. 1; Ezek. 1). It was on a Sunday (this is the earliest mention of Sunday as the Lord's day, as opposed to the Old Testament sabbath) that the Spirit overcame him (cf. Ezek. 2:2; for "in the Spirit" as expressing inspiration cf. Matt. 22:43, variant reading), and the word of the Lord came to him. There was a voice, piercing and resonant as a trumpet (a signal instrument rather than a musical instrument in Biblical usage) **11** which bade him inscribe his vision in a book and so make the words of his prophecy profitable (cf. 2 Tim. 3:16) for the seven churches of the province of Asia. "Seven," the number of completeness, marks these seven churches as representative of the whole church (cf., e. g., 2:7); all seven of the churches mentioned lay on a Roman road, so that distribution of the book from them to neighboring towns and regions would be feasible and convenient; all were also Roman assize towns and therefore centers where the cult of the emperor was fostered and the church's loyalty to her Lord might well be put to the test.

12 When the prophet turned to see whence issued that arresting voice, he beheld a scene all light and gleaming splendor. The voice indicated Christ, whose revelation the book of prophecy is. But the prophet beheld Him, first and foremost, in the glory of His church, symbolized by seven golden lampstands (cf. 20). Jesus has kept His promise that He would be with His disciples always (Matt. 28:20) as the One to whom "all authority . . . has been given" (Matt. 28:18). The exalted Christ has been made "head over all things for the church" (Eph. 1:22). The symbolism of the lampstands indicates both that the churches are what Jesus had promised His disciples they should be, "the light of the world" (Matt. 5:14), and also that the light they give is not their own but is derived from Him who is "the light of the world" (John 8:12; cf. Matt. 4:16). Men may behold the present lordship of Christ in His body, the church.

13 The exalted Christ is portrayed in colors of deity derived from the Old Testament. He is "one like a son of man," that comprehensive Representative of the imperiled "saints of the Most High" (Dan. 7:18) and Guarantor of their victory whom Daniel had beheld coming "with the clouds of heaven . . . to the Ancient of Days" and endowed with "dominion and glory and kingdom" (Dan. 7:13-14), a kingdom universal, eternal, and indestructible (Dan. 7:27). The long robe and girdle indicate that He is Priest as well as King (cf. 6; Ex. 28:4). The golden girdle likewise recalls the mysterious Messenger of the vision in Dan. 10, the Revealer of God's goverance of history for His people "in the latter days" (Dan. 10:14), "whose loins were girded with gold of Uphaz" (Dan. 10:5). **14** The whiteness of His head and hair also mark Him as divine, for in Dan. 7:9 whiteness characterizes God, the Ancient of Days. His "eyes . . . like a flame of fire" again recall the mysterious Messenger (Dan. 10:6), **15** as do His "feet . . . like burnished bronze," splendidly inescapable (Dan. 10:6; cf. also the cherubim of Ezek. 1:7). The voice "like the sound of many waters" recalls Ezekiel's vision of the glory of the Lord. (Ezek. 1:24; cf. 43:2)

16 The seven stars in Christ's right hand are a symbol (often found on Roman imperial coins) of world dominion and are a hint of the dominant theme of the book: Christ, not Caesar, is Lord; the eternal dominion is His (6), and He alone can claim man's total devotion, even though His only weapon is the Word. The sharp two-edged sword issuing from His mouth reminds the hearers of the Messiah promised in Isaiah, who "shall smite the earth with the rod of his mouth, and with the breath of his lips he shall slay the wicked" (Is. 11:4) and of the Servant of the Lord in Is. 49, who can boast that the Lord has made His mouth "like a sharp sword" (Is. 49:2). "His face was like the sun shining in full strength." The appearance of the Son of Man means holy war against all opposing human, demonic, and satanic powers; and there can be no doubt about the victory. The blessing spoken on the victor in the holy war at the close of the Song of Deborah shall surely light on Christ:

So perish all thine enemies, O Lord!
But thy friends be like the sun as he rises in his might.
(Judg. 5:31)

17 The prophet was dismayed in the presence of the Son of Man, wholly dismayed at His overpowering majesty, as Gideon once was dismayed in the presence of the Angel of the Lord and as Isaiah cried out when he beheld the King, the Lord of hosts (Judg. 6:22; Is. 6:5); he collapsed before Him as Daniel collapsed before the Messenger of God (Dan. 10:8) and as Ezekiel fell unconscious on his face when he beheld the glory of the Lord (Ezek. 1:28; cf. 2:2). It was the same feeling of sinful inadequacy that moved Peter to cry out to his familiar Master in Galilee: "Depart from me, for I am a sinful man, O Lord." (Luke 5:8)

But the prophet need not collapse in terror before Christ; the whole Gospel of His incredible grace is in the gesture of His healing and blessing hand laid on His servant and in His words, "Fear not," those words so often used to introduce a promise of deliverance in the Old Testament (e. g., Is. 41:10, 13-14), words which the disciples had heard from Jesus' lips when they grew afraid (e. g., Luke 5:10; John 6:20). All that overpowering divine majesty is there for man, not against him. Christ is "the first and the last," even as the father is (cf. 8; 21:6), **18** the living God, who has acted for man's salvation, going into death and through death into unending victorious life in order that those who are His "may have life, and have it abundantly" (John 10:10). The power of death has been broken by Him; the gates of Hades, death's domain, have been opened by Him. He has authority ("keys") over death and death's domain.

19 His words are "words of eternal life" (John 6:68), and He commissions His prophet to write words of eternal life: The visions which the prophet is permitted to see "in the Spirit" (10) are given to him through the Spirit, whom the church confesses as "the Lord, the Giver of life." They have the long perspective on life, concerned with the church's present ("what is") but seeing that present in the light of the church's past and in the light that falls on the present from the promised future. John's use of the Old Testament to illumine and interpret the present situation of the church (cf., e. g., Balaam, 2:14; Jezebel, 2:20) and his emphatic proclamation of God the Creator (4:11; 14:7) illustrate the backward reference of his vision. And what is the message of the whole book but the prophet's summons and encouragement to the church to live *now,* amid her present difficulties and dangers, in the light that shines upon her from the future which God has determined ("what is to take place hereafter")? The prophet dares to bid the church to be *now* the living reality of a new people of God destined to inherit a new world where God makes all things new (21:5). The idea held by many interpreters that "what you see" (which could also be rendered "what you *saw*") refers to the vision of Ch. 1 and that "what is" refers to the content of Chs. 2 and 3 and "what is to take place hereafter" refers to the succeeding visions is attractive but hardly does justice to the fact that past, present, and future are components in all the visions. **20** They all spell eternal life, these visions. For as surely as the eternal dominion is Christ's, it is the eternal dominion of His kingly and priestly servants (6); as surely as the seven stars of universal dominion are in Christ's right hand (16), so surely shall they who are kings and priests, men ransomed "for God from every tribe and tongue and people and nation" also "reign on earth." (5:9-10)

That is the "mystery," the secret reality to be known only by revelation (cf. Matt. 13:11), of the seven churches, those seven lampstands whose borrowed flame is continually threatened by satanic gusts and, to all seeming, is about to splutter and die (cf. 2:5)—but for all that, in reality "angels," servitors and messengers of God who will surely triumph in the triumph of God and Christ.

The Letters to the Seven Churches
2:1—3:22

In the (formally almost identical) letters to the churches Christ, speaking through His Spirit by the written word of His prophet, *first* bids the prophet write; *second,* He identifies Himself, usually by some feature of the inaugural vision (1:9-20); *third,* He addresses the church in its Godward aspect as "angel of the church" (cf. 1:20), with words of diagnosis (praise or blame) and exhortation; *fourth,* He warns every hearer to give heed to the inspired word (in four of the letters this call to vigilant attention stands in fifth place, 2:29; 3:6, 13, 22); and *fifth,* He promises to "him who conquers" a participation in His own victory and its everlasting fruits.

The Letter to Ephesus
2:1-7

1 Ephesus was the chief city of the Roman province of Asia, of high political, commercial, religious (cf. Acts 19:27, 35), and cultural importance; there is therefore an inner fitness in the fact that Christ here identifies Himself, in the face of this imposing power and influence, as the Holder of the seven stars, the Wielder of a worldwide dominion before which even Ephesus grows insignificant, and as the vigilant Patroller ("walks among") of His churches (cf. 1:20); His strength is theirs, wherever they may be, and their responsibility is to Him.

2 He praises the church, first, for being faithful in that responsibility. The men of Ephesus have remembered the words of their Lord and of Paul their apostle (Matt. 7:15-20; Acts 20:28-31); there lives in their faith that active, toilsome aversion to evil men which is the hallmark of men who await their Lord's return and in the strength of their hope and in the expection of hearing a "well done" (Matt. 25:21) from His lips can endure the toil which fidelity to Him entails. They have borne the burden of truth, have endeavored to "test everything" and "hold fast what is good" (1 Thess. 5:21), and have not shunned the pain of calling false apostles false and of rejecting them as messengers of Satan disguised as angels of light (2 Cor. 11:13-15). **3** They have sought to endure for the sake of Him whose name they bear (cf. James 2:7) and have not grown weary in enduring.

4 But in this necessary conflict with evil men and false teaching they have let slip from them, have "abandoned," that which evinces them as sons of their heavenly Father (Matt. 5:45), that first love engendered in them by the Christ who interceded for His enemies (Luke 23:34). They behold that causeless love in Him even now; He will not abandon them, though they abandon Him. He woos them still, bidding them remember, as the Lord once bade Jerusalem remember

> . . . the devotion of your youth,
> your love as a bride. (Jer. 2:2)

5 Remembering, recalling and reliving the Gospel, will enable them to repent and believe; and in repentance and faith they will be enabled to love as they loved at first, with the love of Him who loved them and freed them for a life of love "by His blood" (1:6). This they can do, and this they must do, for their existence as church depends on their so doing. How can a church that has abandoned love continue to serve as His lampstand who as God's spoken Word of love is the Light of the world? (cf. John 1:4, 14-17). The Lord will remove that lampstand from its place. "From him who has not, even what he has will be taken away" (Matt. 13:12).

6 The Lord's word of reproach does not cancel out His previous word of praise. Love can and must coexist in the repentant heart with the will to defend and maintain the truth. The Ephesians can and must hate the *works,* the pretensions and lies, of the Nicolaitans, men who pretended to apostolic authority (2) and with their lies led the people of God into a licentious compromise with surrounding paganism (14-15); but they can share their Lord's holy aversion to false pretensions and licentious lies and yet hold unswervingly to the course of selfless love which He has walked before them and for them.

7 The Spirit is the completion of the presence of Christ; Christ can therefore demand for the Spirit's word the same vigilant hearing which He demanded for His own words in the days of His flesh (e. g., Matt. 11:15; 13:9, 43), a hearing that is a hearing-and-doing in one (cf. Matt. 7:24-27). The Lord's last word to Ephesus is one of promise, not of threat. He will give to the faithful who in the impending tribulation (cf. 9) follow Him into His death and into His victory that everlasting life with God in man's true home, Paradise, from which man was shut out when he first listened to the lie and lusted after forbidden fruit. (Gen. 3:22-24)

The Letter to Smyrna
2:8-11

8 The angel of the church (the church in its Godward aspect) is addressed by Christ and is bidden to *be* what by virtue of Christ's death and resurrection she has become and can be. The church needs the help of Him who is "the first and the last" (Christ shares with His Father the eternal glory of being "the Alpha and the Omega" of all history, 1:8); the church needs the help of Him who has won the victory over death and wills to share that victory with His own. (Cf. 1:17-18)

9 For the church in Smyrna has none of the glory of the city of Smyrna; she has only the wealth of the poor whom God has chosen, "to be rich in faith" (James 2:5). The church's tribulation stands in sharp contrast to Smyrna's political good fortune; Caesar smiled on the city that was proud to be a center of the imperial cult, but Caesar frowned darkly on the sect that would not compromise its loyalty to the Lord Jesus by offering a pinch of incense at the emperor's statue and acknowledging him as Lord. And the numerous Jews of Smyrna allied themselves with Caesar against the church. Then (A.D. 95) as later in the time of Polycarp (A.D. 155) they committed themselves to Satan's lie and to Satan's murderous will (cf. John 8:44). Thus they rejected anew their own Messiah and forfeited their right to be called the people of God and became the synagog of Satan.

10 But the strong word of Christ, His "Fear not!" which had fortified His apostles on their first venture into hostile Judaism (Matt. 10:26, 28, 31), is still the sole and sufficient assurance of His church. The church is destined to suffer, as Christ had foretold (Matt. 10:16-23, 34-39), and the will of those who cause her suffering is a satanic will; the devil inspires his synagog (9) to inflict imprisonment and death on the church. But the church has an armor of triple brass to keep her unafraid: She is to know that her Lord has not forgotten her. Satan no doubt intends her suffering as a temptation, but God designs it as a test; she is being tested as once believing Abraham was tested (Gen. 22), and the believing church knows that God's testing, being His way of making His people perfect and complete, is cause for joy (James 1:2-4). Also, she is not being merely abandoned to the freaks of satanic malice; her Lord has set limits ("ten days") to her tribulation. In the power of the Lord's word she can find strength to "be faithful unto death"; His blessing on those who endure persecution for His sake (Matt. 5:10-12) will follow her into imprisonment and dying.

11 If she will but heed the voice of the Spirit now addressing her, she will share the victory of the Conqueror of death (cf. 1:17-18) and lose her life in order to gain it. She will by dying gain a life that is proof against the horror of "the second death," that final, definitive separation from God and life (cf. Matt. 10:28) described in 20:14 and 21:8 as unending torment in the lake of fire.

12-13 Pergamum had many claims to distinction; it was, since the second century before Christ, capital of the Roman province of Asia and was renowned for its library, which rivaled the famous library of Alexandria and has left a monument to that fame in our word "parchment" (derived from "Pergamum"). It was, moreover, a great religious center, famous as a seat of Asclepius, the Greek god of healing, possessing a magnificently sculptured altar dedicated to Zeus, to mention only two outstanding examples of its pagan religiosity; and it was fervidly devoted to the cult of the Roman emperor. It was probably this last feature which led the prophet to call the city the place "where Satan's throne is." Here, where men were eager to acclaim the Roman emperor as "Lord and God," the satanic lie held royal sway in the hearts of men; here, too, the satanic will to destroy what the lie cannot ensnare had already struck a deadly blow to those who held fast the name of Jesus and would call none other "Lord and God" but Him. The "hour of trial" destined to come "on the whole world" (3:10) has already come to Pergamum. Yet the church has held fast to the name of Jesus even in the face of threatening death and has not denied her faith in Him. Indeed, one of her number, Antipas (otherwise unknown), has sealed his testimony with his blood and has followed the faithful Witness (1:5) into death and victory. The church has need of Him "who has the sharp two-edged sword" of the Messiah and can wage war for her (cf. 2:16) both against satanic power and against the satanic lie.

14 The church needs help both against enemies without and against enemies within. There are those in the church at Pergamum who would persuade the church to follow the way of accommodation and compromise, as Balaam had once taught Israel to compromise with the lascivious worship of Baal Peor (Num. 31:15-16; cf. 25:1-2). Why give offense to our pagan townsmen and kinsfolk, these men might argue, by scrupling to eat of the "food sacrificed to idols" set before them at so many civic and social occasions? (cf. 1 Cor. 8—10). Why attempt to maintain an ideal of sexual purity which public opinion (and even some religious feeling) would brand as an inexplicable whim of eccentric rigor? (cf. 1 Peter 4:3-4). Would not a slight slackening, an insignificant compromise, keep all placid and serene and improve the public position of the church?

15 Such were the teachings of the Nicolaitans. The group is known really only from these notices in The Revelation to John (2:6, 15); there is little or nothing to connect them with the Nicolaus of Acts 6:5. Thus far the men of the church of Pergamum have not followed their lead; but they have tolerated the men who put stumbling-blocks in the way of helpless "little ones" who believe in Jesus, an offense so terrible that Jesus would only hint at the punishment of the offender: "It would be better for him to have a great millstone fastened round his neck and to be drowned in the depth of the sea." (Matt. 18:6)

16 The Nicolaitan error is not just another phenomenon in ecclesiastical history, to be discussed and classified and tolerated; a genuine love which holds fast to what is good and hates what is evil (Rom. 12:9) will "hate the works of the Nicolaitans," as they are hated by the vigilant Lord of the church (6). The "tolerant" church is therefore called upon to repent, to turn in holy aversion from that which will soon invoke the avenging sword of the dread Warrior, the Lord of the church (12), in holy war against those "who hold the teaching of the Nicolaitans." (15)

17 That is what the Spirit, Author of love (cf. Rom. 15:30), is saying to the churches now. That is the way to victory, and to the victor the victorious Christ promises paradise: He will give to him who overcomes the satanic lie and defies the satanic threat of murder "the hidden manna" (lost, according to Judaic popular belief, when the temple was destroyed, but hidden by Jeremiah and to be restored to the people of God in the days of the Messiah), the food of paradise; and, as an amulet against all harm, he will give "a white stone" inscribed with the name above all names which only the eyes of faith can decipher—faith can see in the Crucified the Warrior with the two-edged sword who shall topple the throne of Satan in illustrious Pergamum and all other hostile thrones as well.

44

Just what the "white stone" (called an amulet above) refers to can hardly be determined precisely. Some interpreters take it to mean a token which admits the bearer to a banquet or feast. This would fit the context well: The faithful Christian who forgoes the pleasurable feasts of the Nicolaitans shall find his reward in being admitted to the feasts of Paradise, by virtue of the name which he has kept holy. (Cf. 1 Peter 3:15)

The Letter to Thyatira
2:18-29

18 Compared with Ephesus, Smyrna, and Pergamum Thyatira was a small and inglorious town. But it was a town of great commercial importance, and inscriptions attest the presence of many trade guilds in the city. How the Gospel first came to Thyatira we do not know. The founding of the church there probably dates from the time of Paul's ministry in Ephesus (A.D. 52—55) when "all the residents of Asia heard the word of the Lord." (Acts 19:10)

19 That word had not returned empty, and "The Son of God," whose fiery vision (18) searches even the minds and hearts of men (23), is warm in His commendation of the church's love, which issued in Christlike service (cf. Matt. 20:28), and of her faith, which enabled her to endure patiently "in hope . . . against hope" (Rom. 4:18) and to grow in active love and enduring faith even as she endured; she abounded "more and more" (1 Thess. 4:1, 10) in the works which her Lord approved.

20 But she shares with Pergamum (cf. 14) the guilt of tolerating what she cannot, in her love and faith, approve. She tolerates a woman who claims prophetic authority for her teaching; the Spirit likens her to Jezebel, Ahab's Phoenician queen, who corrupted the faith of Israel with "the harlotries and the sorceries" of her native gods, Baal and Astarte (2 Kings 9:22; cf. 1 Kings 16:31-33). She resembles the Balaamlike teachers of Pergamum (14), the Nicolaitans (15), in advocating a compromise with paganism and beguiling the Lord's servants "to practice immorality and to eat food sacrificed to idols." The civic complexion of Thyatira as a city of trade-guilds suggests that it was participation in the

45

trade-guilds that made the compromise attractive and prompted the beguilements. In Thyatira one had to belong to a trade-guild in order to live and grow rich; belonging to a trade-guild meant participating in the guild's common meals, with their libations and sacrifices to a pagan god and, frequently, their concomitant festival excesses of alcohol and sex. A man must live, and the temptation to do in Thyatira what the Thyatirans do must have been strong, and the compromise could be made to appear a reasonable one.

21 The Lord has called the would-be prophetess to repentance (by what means does not appear), but she has refused to repent of her immorality (literally, "fornication"; she is inducing the church to become unfaithful to her Lord and to go awhoring after other gods) and, for her, the time for repentance is over. **22** Under the judgment of the Lord, who inevitably advances with brazen feet against her, her bed of adulterous luxury will become her bed of pain. Those who have flirted with her seductive teaching will come into great afflication unless they repent. For them the time of repentance is not yet over. **23** It is over for her "children," for those who have inherited from her her willful and stubborn bent of apostasy. They will be punished by a death which is a dreadful witness to the Lord "who searches mind and heart"; all the churches shall come to know Him as the inescapable Judge, who sees and appraises all deeds in their true light and gives to each man as his works deserve.

24 Upon the rest, who have resisted the prophetess' beguiling invitation to explore "the deep things of Satan" (which she and her followers probably called "the depths of God," cf. 1 Cor. 2:10), the Lord has no punitive burden to impose. **25** He simply bids them live as ever in their great Taskmaster's eye until He comes to give them their due reward.

26 The reward for him who overcomes with Christ will be great. The man whose works are the works of the Christ, genuine fruit of the true vine (cf. John 15:1-8), will share in the triumph of the Christ as that triumph is pictured in Ps. 2:8-9. He shall share in His power **27** and in His shattering triumph over all who oppose His reign. **28** Christ will give to

His faithful ones all that He Himself has received from the Father (cf. Matt. 11:27; 28:18). He will give Himself, the first light of God's new day (cf. 22:16) that is breaking upon the world. **29** Once more we hear the demand to heed the Spirit's voice.

The Letter to Sardis
3:1-6

1 The Lord who addresses the church in Sardis has universal dominion. He holds "the seven stars" in His right hand (cf. 1:16; 2:1). He has, moreover, "the seven spirits of God" (cf. 1:4), the plenitude of the Spirit of God "who gives life to the dead and calls into existence the things that do not exist" (Rom. 4:17), the plenitude of the Spirit who can give breath and life to the bleached bones of the dead people of God (cf. Ezek. 37:14). His word can speak life to the sleeping saints of Sardis and call them back from the grave.

The easy somnolence of Sardis is worse and more dangerous than that lulled sense of security which had overtaken the men of Sardis in the past. They had trusted in the strength of their impregnable citadel and had twice (in 540 B.C. and 218 B.C.) seen their citadel fall into enemy hands while they "slept." The sleep of the church of Sardis is the sleep of death and only **2** the "Awake!" of Him who roused up Lazarus four days dead can avail to rouse them. Sardis had peace. We hear of no attack from the "synagogue of Satan" (2:9) in Sardis; no throne of Satan (2:13) was set up there to challenge the sole sovereignty of the throne of God (cf. 4:2). No "deep things of Satan" (2:24) lured them away with the seduction of a Balaam (2:14) or a Jezebel (2:20) from the salubrious "depths of God" (1 Cor. 2:10). The church in Sardis "had peace" (Acts 9:31), but she did not put that peace to the use for which God intended it; she was not "built up," and instead of "walking in the fear of the Lord" (Acts 9:31) and quietly fulfilling the duties of her peaceful lot she took color from her surroundings in luxurious and lazy Sardis. The church was not "multiplied" (Acts 9:31); men of Sardis are "on the point of death"; they must needs be roused to the wakeful ministry of love with which they might strengthen their moribund brethren. Their Lord has not found their works "perfect"; the works which God has prepared beforehand for His new creation to walk in have not been carried out. They are not "perfect," literally, not "fulfilled"; the word of God that was to make them perfect in word and work has returned empty to mock the Speaker of the word. And God is not mocked with impunity.

3 And yet the Lord of the seven stars does not begin with threatening. He begins with a renewal of His first promise: "Remember!" He bids them recall with thanksgiving, confession, and praise the light which first raised them from the dead (cf. Eph. 5:14; Acts 26:23) and to "keep that"; repent and walk, He bids them, in the light that has been given you (cf. John 12:35-36); walk in the light while the light still shines, for the night comes when the Lord, who still promises and proffers His blessing, will come with incalculable suddenness, "like a thief" (cf. Matt. 24:43), for judgment.

4 The church in Sardis is not yet ripe for judgment; there are still those who know what hour has struck (Rom. 13:11), who know that it is time to be robed in a clean wedding garment, lest the King be offended by the presence of a guest who presumes to come to His feast in smutched secularity (Matt. 22:11-14). They who even now "believe in the light," who have "become sons of light," and walk in the light (John 12:35-36) shall be forever with their Lord, wearing the white garments of festive joy and victory.

5 Those who, like them ("thus"), remember what they have received and keep it and repent (3) shall be the conquerors, the white-robed victors whose names will not be expunged from the book of life (cf. Ex. 32:32; Ps. 69:28). Their names will be written in the citizen-rolls of the eternal city of God. For the Son of God, who has all authority in heaven and earth (cf. 1), will acknowledge them before God and all the company of heaven as He has promised. (Matt. 10:32)

6 It is the Spirit of truth who takes what is Christ's and declares it to the churches. To Him the churches must listen when He warns of death and when He promises life.

The Letter to Philadelphia
3:7-13

7 The Lord's words to the church in Philadelphia are all

approbation; no shadow of reproof or blame falls on her. But these words are not words of easy or facile approbation; they are the words of One who styles Himself "the holy one, the true one," with titles of God the unerring Judge Himself (cf. 6:10). He has "the key of David" and can, as was the case with Hezekiah's steward Eliakim (Is. 22:22), admit men to the King or exclude them from the King's presence, according to His faithful judgment. His approbation means admission to the kingdom of God.

8 He knows the "works" of Philadelphia, and He has provided for the church of Philadelphia "an open door which no one is able to shut." What are the "works" that are to have so high a reward? There is nothing mightily heroic to report on this church that has "but little power." The faithful of Philadelphia are blessed because they come under Jesus' benediction: "Blessed . . . are those who hear the word of God and keep it!" (Luke 11:28); they have kept the word of their Lord, and that word has given them the "patient endurance" (10) to confess His name before hostile men.

9 The hostile men here, as in Smyrna (2:9), are Jews who have belied and forfeited their Old Testament name as "assembly of the Lord" and have become "the synagogue of Satan" by persecuting the Messiah and His faithful ones. The holy and true Lord will overcome their hostility. The ancient promises made to Israel will be fulfilled in a strange way; whereas Isaiah had foretold that foreigners would capitulate to Israel and recognize Israel's God (Is. 43:4; 45:14; 49:23; 60:14; cf. Ps. 86:9), it is now ancient Israel that will bow down before the new Israel, "the Israel of God" (Gal. 6:16), and confess that the elective love of God has reached out to include men "from every tribe and tongue and people and nation." (5:9)

10 As for the church: "With the loyal thou dost show thyself loyal . . . thou dost deliver a humble people" (Ps. 18:25, 27), the psalmist sang of Israel's Lord. The church has kept her Lord's word (8) and has, in the strength of it, patiently endured; the Lord will keep this church; amid all those successive waves of preliminary judgments of God, each more severe than the last (cf. chs. 6—9), which shall sweep and sift the world, the church shall be safely kept. (Cf. 7:1-8)

49

11 Beyond those preliminary "trials" there looms the return of the church's Lord for the last judgment. It will not be long delayed ("I am coming soon") and need hold no terrors for the faithful church. The quiet fidelity that has preserved her hitherto will preserve her then; she need but hold fast to what she has, that no insidious or hostile hand may snatch from her the prize already won for her by Christ.

12 The Lord's gift to the conqueror is described in terms that would be familiar to the men of Philadelphia: In Philadelphia one who had served his city honorably and well was honored by having an inscribed pillar set up in one of the temples to commemorate his services. The One holy and true will reward His own, not with a stone column dedicated to his memory in an earthly temple which an earthquake (such as were frequent in Philadelphia) might move from its place but with a place from which he cannot be moved, in the temple of God. There he will *be* a serving and supporting column, a living, functioning part of the living whole (cf. Eph. 2:20-22), inscribed with the very name of God and so marked as His inviolable own, inscribed with the name of the new city of God, which reads: "The Lord is there" (Ezek. 48:35), inscribed with Christ's new name, that new name above all names before which every knee shall bow amid the acclamation of an adoring universe. (Phil. 2:10-11)

13 Now is the time when that great prize is won or lost; now let the churches hear and heed the Spirit's voice.

The Letter to Laodicea
3:14-22

14 The Lord speaks to the church of Laodicea as One who stands wholly on the side of God. He is in person "the Amen," the Affirmation and Confirmation of all God's promises (cf. 2 Cor. 1:20), the royally valid "witness" to God (cf. John 18:37) who has been with Him from the beginning as the Prime Source of all creation. (Cf. John 1:1-3; Col. 1:15)

15-16 He is witness to both "the kindness and the severity of God" (Rom. 11:22); a faithful witness must witness both, as the record of Jesus in the gospels makes plain. His words to Laodicea embody both the sharpest rebuke and the warmest encouragement and promise in all the seven letters. The rebuke: The church of Laodicea is "lukewarm"; whatever the Laodiceans may have been in earlier, happier days when Paul's forceful preaching caused all Asia to hear the Word of the Lord (Acts 19:10), they have since become tepidly casual Christians, a nauseous abomination destined to be spat out of the mouth of the Lord who claims men wholly by His love and cannot abide men who "go limping with two different opinions" (1 Kings 18:21). **17** They are complacent and self-satisfied, moreover, these wealthy citizens of a wealthy town, and have no eyes for their own wretched state of ill-clad, blind beggary.

18-19 So blind are they that the Witness to the kindness of God must remind them that even His severity is the kindness of a loving Father, who exposes and convicts and disciplines them because He loves them (cf. Prov. 3:12; Heb. 12:5-11). Only one who has God's creative omnipotence can offer the advice which He offers: to buy "without money and without price" (Is. 55:1) finer gold of greater value than wealthy Laodicea ever had, coin of God's own realm; white clothing of the celestial, blessed ones, able to cover the evil nakedness that shames them in the sight of God; an eye salve more effective than the one compounded by the famous medics of Laodicea, to give men eyes for both the severity and the kindness of God. Their Creator Lord can give what He demands; His Spirit can make fervent men of these lukewarm saints (cf. Rom. 12:11). As in the Old Testament, so in the New: The Lord can turn the hearts of His people back. (Cf. 1 Kings 18:37)

20 The Witness who calls to repentance pleads for His people's return with warm and winning words; He would be their guest and stands knocking for admission at each man's door. If a man will heed His wooing voice, He will come in and they shall dine together in the leisurely fellowship of the evening meal.

21 The conqueror is he who allows himself to be conquered by the Guest who knocks on the door and permits His condescending love to rouse him from the lukewarm torpor of his uncommitted life. The Lord is not satisfied merely to condescend; He wills also to exalt the lukewarm blind and naked beggar to Himself. He promises him a part in His own victory over death (cf. 1:18), coenthronement with Himself at God's right hand.

22 How does one rise from Laodicea's abominated (16) depths to such a height? How does one follow the Crucified into death and into the glory of the Conqueror? One need but listen to the Spirit's voice, and gold and clothing and healing, companionship with God's Son, and enthronement with the Son are freely his.

The Second Vision: The Seven Seals
4:1—7:17

The first vision (1:9—3:22) has made clear to the churches who (or rather, *whose*) they are and where they stand. They stand in a world imperiled by "the synagogue of Satan" (2:9; 3:9) and the throne of Satan (2:13), on the brink of "the deep things of Satan" (2:24). But they belong to Him who says, "Behold I am alive for evermore" (1:18); they stand on the brink of eternal life (2:7, 11; 3:5). Therefore no compromise is necessary or possible. That is the real "what is" (1:19), as the Spirit reveals reality. But (the persistent question of "men of little faith," Matt. 6:30-33) what about tomorrow, what of the future, "the hour of trial which is coming on the whole world" (3:10)? What of "what is to take place hereafter" (1:19)? Dare we, can we be the same uncompromisingly loyal men there that we are now, under the praise, rebuke, and encouragement of our Lord? To this question the vision of the seven seals gives answer.

Our God Reigns and Lives Forever
4:1-11

1 The answer begins with a formula often used by John to mark a vision as of especial solemnity and significance ("After this I looked," cf. 7:1; 7:9; 15:5; 18:1). The prophet sees "an open door" in heaven (cf. Ezek. 1:1). Only God can open God's doors, whether it be the door to the kingdom (3:8) or the door which gives a glimpse of the future, as here; He gives access to His throne room to which the door in heaven opens. The same trumpet voice which bade John write the word of God to the churches (1:10-11) now bids him, in terms reminiscent of the Lord's command to Moses at Sinai (Ex.

19:24), come into His presence and see what He has determined ("must") for His people's future.

2 Again the Spirit enclosed him (cf. 1:10), and under that inspiration the prophet beholds a throne, and "one seated on the throne." "One seated on the throne" may seem a pale, if reverential, designation for God. But for one who lives with the Old Testament, as the prophet evidently did (of the 404 verses of Revelation, 278 are reminiscent of the OT) and as his readers apparently did too, the phrase evokes colorful associations of kingly majesty and might. The prophets Isaiah, Ezekiel, and Daniel beheld God ("the King, the Lord of hosts," Is. 6:5; "the glory of the Lord," Ezek. 1:28; the "ancient of days," Dan. 7:9) seated on His throne in heaven. The psalms ring with adoration of Him who is seated upon His throne and reigns (e. g., Ps. 22:3; 47:8; 80:1; 103:19). Ps. 29 crowns its ecstatic hymn on the "glory and strength" of the Lord, whose powerful and majestic voice moves thunderously upon the waters, breaks the cedars of Lebanon, makes solid mountains skip like frisky calves, flashes forth flames of fire, shakes the silent immovable wilderness, makes the oaks to whirl and strips forests bare—crowns that terrifying picture with the words:

The Lord sits *enthroned* over the flood;
The Lord sits *enthroned as king* forever (Ps. 29:10).

Him whom even the rebellious flood that spits into the face of heaven must obey, Him His people can trust; to Him they can pray:

May the Lord give strength to his people!
May the Lord bless his people with peace! (Ps. 29:11)

3 To Him the new people of God, too, can pray for the blessing of peace, for though He dwells in an "unapproachable light" (1 Tim. 6:16) like that of greenly flashing jasper and the deep luster of red carnelian, and is sundered from all creatures by "a sea of glass" (6), there is about His throne an emerald rainbow; the rainbow is the abiding symbol of God's covenant with all flesh after the Flood (Gen. 9:8-17). That same symbol had appeared to Ezekiel in his vision of the glory of the Lord (Ezek. 1:28) when judgment loomed over old Israel. Now as then the rainbow signifies that the God of judgment (indicated by the throne, 2, 4-6) is still the God of the covenant, the God of compassionate forbearance, and will in the midst of wrath remember mercy.

4 The mercy of God is attested also by the presence of the "twenty-four elders" in His throne room. Their number is a multiple of 12, and multiples of 12 recall God's Israel, the 12 tribes (cf. 7:4-8; 21:12, 14). The 24 elders, enthroned, golden-crowned, clad in the white garments of purity, festivity, and victory, represent the people of God as they are in God's intent, as His new creation in Christ, made alive, raised up, seated in heavenly places (cf. Eph. 1:20), and glorified (Rom. 8:30). (Some interpreters think of the 24 elders as a superior class of angels, close to God and familiar with His counsels, cf. 5:6; 7:13, distinguished both from the rest of the heavenly host, 5:11; 7:11, and from the transfigured saints, 7:13; 14:3. In the number 24 they see a reflection of the 24 classes of priests and Levites, 1 Chron. 24 and 25, and see the closest parallel in the "elders" of Is. 24:23, the heavenly council before whom the Lord of hosts "will manifest his glory" when He shall judge the nations.)

5 "The Lord reigns; let the peoples tremble!" (Ps. 99:1), for from His throne issue those tokens of His terrible majesty that once made His people tremble at Sinai (Ex. 19:16; cf. Ezek. 1:13; Ps. 18:7-15; 77:18; Job 37:1-5, 15, 21-24). "The Lord reigns; let the earth rejoice" (Ps. 97:1), for His Spirit is before the throne, seven torches of fire whose incessant motion, fostering warmth, and outstreaming light symbolize God's active, benign, and creative will to communion with His people, the seven churches. (Cf. 1:4)

6 To behold God enthroned is no light thing (cf. Is. 6:5); only God Himself can create communion between Himself and His creatures. Only He can reach across the crystalline sea which otherwise bars all creation from access to His holiness. He *has* reached out; He is mindful still of the covenant of the bow (3) by which He has bound Himself to refrain from judgment upon "every living creature" (Gen. 9:10) on earth until His mercy shall have had full room and scope to work.

And so it is that creation, symbolized by the "four living creatures" (cf. Ezek. 1:5, 10) surrounds His throne and stands in His service continually vigilant ("full of eyes," 8) to perform His will. **7** There stands the lordly power of the lion, the solid serviceable strength of the ox, the skill and intelligence of man (one with creation in his fall and one in destined glory, cf. Rom. 8:19-23), and the unwearied speed of the soaring eagle (cf. Is. 40:31); the glory of the seraphim (Is. 6:2) and of the cherubim (cf. Ezek. 1:5-14) decks out restored creation.

8 The living creatures will be active in the execution of God's counsels (6:1, 3, 5, 7); but their first and constant business is to sing and to adore. John hears again the thrice-holy of the seraphim which Isaiah heard in the year that king Uzziah died (Is. 6:1-3). These representatives of all created beings acclaim the Lord God Almighty, whose will and work must and will prevail, as the Thrice Holy One, the wholly Other before whose pure otherness impure man must quail and despair (cf. Is. 6:5) and even the seraphim shroud their creaturehood by covering their face and feet as they wait upon Him (Is. 6:2) at whose voice the foundations of His temple quake (Is. 6:4), whose ponderous majesty overwhelmingly fills the earth (Is. 6:3). He it is who "is to come"; "what must soon take place" (1:1; cf. 1:19) will be the work of His will, His alone; His kingdom comes.

9 When the four living creatures thus ascribe ("give") to Him His proper glory and give to Him the honor and thanksgiving, hitherto denied Him by sinful man (Rom. 1:21), due to the King who lives forever (cf. Dan. 7:27; 12:7), **10** the church joins the created beings in obeisance and doxology. The 24 elders cast down before the throne their crowns of victory, in token that the glory of their victory belongs to Him who is seated upon the throne; their victory is the gift of His grace. **11** They ascribe to the Creator the name which the emperor Domitian has usurped, "our Lord and God," the name which He along deserves as the Alpha and Omega who will in these last days take up His Creator-power and reign (cf. 7:12; 11:16-17; 12:10) in undisputed glory and honor.

The church is to know and remember when she hears the words of prophecy which tell her of coming conflict and fearful judgments that the God in whom she believes is enthroned in heaven and that He (not Satan, not Antichrist, not any power of this world) is in charge and "in everything words for good with those who love him" (Rom. 8:28). Amid all the hell-let-loose that surrounds and threatens her she is to remember this; her business now is the heavenly business of filling God's throne room with adoration and praise.

Christus Has Conquered:
The Slain Lamb Takes the Scroll with Seven Seals
5:1-14

The vision of God royally enthroned (Ch. 4) is a pictorial restatement of Jesus' opening proclamation: "The kingdom of God is at hand" (Mark 1:15). There are hints even here, in the rainbow encircling God's throne, in the adoring presence of the elders who represent the church victorious, and in their acclamation of "our Lord and God" that the coming-in of God's royal reign in these last days not only spells "repent" (turn and unite your will with His) but must be accompanied by an act of God which makes possible the glad imperative "believe in the gospel" (Mark 1:15). That act and the good news of it are the theme of Ch. 5.

1 The prophet sees in the right hand of God a scroll. John's readers would know from Ezek. 2:8—3:3 that the scroll contains the counsels of God; the fact that the scroll is inscribed within and without indicates that the counsels of God in their fulness (all that the succeeding visions are to reveal) are meant. The seven seals mark the document as official, perhaps as a last will and testament (cf. Heb. 9:15-17), not to be taken by any hand unauthorized nor to be looked into by any prying eyes. God's counsels are His own, His secret, which He alone reveals (cf. Matt. 13:11: "To you *it has been given to know* the secrets").

2 A strong angel (probably Gabriel, whose name means "the strong one of God"; for Gabriel's connection with visions, cf. Dan. 8:16; 9:21) utters the question: "Who is the man to reveal and execute the counsels of God?" The opening of the sealed scroll signifies (as the sequel shows, 6:1, 3, 5, etc.) both the making-known *and* the execution of God's will.

3 There is no man; the whole universe in all its divisions (cf. Ex. 20:4; Phil. 2:10) answers the challenge with the creation's stricken silence of impotence. **4** The prophet weeps as it is borne in on him how powerless all human wisdom and power is over against the unknown and unknowable future. If no one be found to answer the angel's challenge, mankind and mankind's world have no future and no hope (cf. Jer. 29:11). The bright world into which the prophet has been allowed to gaze (Ch. 4) will remain forever hidden and remote, a place which a man may dream of perhaps but cannot ever attain.

5 But one of the elders, a member of the bright company of those who walk by sight and no longer in the dark by faith (cf. 2 Cor. 5:7), bids him cease his weeping; there is One who has conquered (3:21) sin (1:5-6) and death and lives forever (1:17-18) in that world where the record of the hope of man is legible and known. He can open the scroll and look into it, for He is "the Lion of the tribe of Judah" whom dying Jacob beheld from afar, winning the obedience of the peoples not only by His might but also by the abundant peaceable blessings of milk and wine (Gen. 49:10-12); He is the Root of Jesse of whom Isaiah spoke, upon whom the Spirit of the Lord was to rest in fulness (Is. 11:1-2; cf. John 1:32), that He might in the Spirit's power be the King whom God desired for His people, girt in righteousness and faithfulness (Is. 11:3-5), and might fill the earth in which all "shall be full of the knowledge of the Lord" with paradisal peace. (Is. 11:6-9)

6 But He who is to end the weeping hopelessness of the world (as it finds expression in the prophet's tears, 4-5) is, to all seeming, neither the heroic Conqueror foretold by Jacob (Gen. 49) nor the charismatic King of whom Isaiah sang (Is. 11) but a lamb, no king but a servant and a sacrifice (Is. 53:10), who still bears on His body the mark of His redeeming sacrifice (cf. 9),

> Rich wounds, yet visible above
> In beauty glorified.

The Crucified is the Victor; He stands at the center of the throne room of God the King, the Servant who has gained life by losing it (Matt. 16:25; 10:38-39) and has become the Servant "exalted and lifted up and . . . very high," at whose appearance kings shut their mouths and cease to prate of glory and power (Is. 52:13, 15). The seven horns of omnipotence (cf. Num. 23:22; Deut. 33:17; Ps. 75) are His, and so are the eyes of omniscience—the seven spirits of God sent out into the world to do His proper revealing and saving work are the eyes wherewith the Lamb looks upon His ransomed world; the Spirit who shall guide men into all the truth is His to give (John 16:7, 13). **7** He can cross the glassy sea which separates creation from the Creator and can take from His right hand the scroll whereon is written the future of the world.

8-14 That act, whereby the Christ takes up His power and reigns, evokes a threefold chorus of praise; the song begins with those nearest the throne, the four living creatures and the 24 elders; thence it moves out to include the myriads of the angelic host; and finally it is taken up by "every creature in heaven and on earth," who pay like obeisance to God on the throne and to the Lamb. The ecumenical service of praise closes with creation's Amen and the prostrate adoration of the church.

8 Man and nature, no longer at strife, unite in doxology; and the worship of the saints above is one with that of the saints below—the prayers of the church on earth, symbolized by the golden bowls full of incense (cf. Ps. 141:2) are brought before the Lamb by the ministration of the 24 elders of the heavenly court. As surely as the Lamb rules the world, "the world," as Luther once said, "is ruled by the prayers of the saints."

9 Amid the music of harps and the wafting of clouds of incense, the "new song" celebrating the new and ultimate divine victory (cf. Ps. 96:1; Is. 42:10) is heard. It is a doxological elaboration, as it were, of the words in which Jesus had once described His mission: "Whoever would be first among you must be your slave; even as the Son of man came not to be served but to serve, and to give his life as a ransom for many" (Matt. 20:27-28). He who now has in His hand the destinies of all creation has that power and authority because He came to serve and expended Himself in that service, even to the shedding of His redeeming blood, thus paying the ransom that liberated doomed and desolate men and set them free for God—He died, Peter says, "that he might bring us to God" (1 Peter 3:18). He gave His life "a ransom for many" (Matt. 20:28); the new song vividly expands that "many"—all men, whether united by ties of a common descent ("tribes") or of a common language ("tongues") or of a common history and constitution ("people") or of common customs and mores ("nations"), all have been set free by the Lamb and His sacrifice **10** with a freedom that makes of them kings and priests, to share His everlasting reign on earth.

11 The song swells as the "myriads of myriads" of angels (once seen by Daniel in attendance on the Ancient of Days, Dan. 7:10) take it up. **12** To the Victor-Victim they ascribe wealth and wisdom, inexhaustible resources and the wit to use them rightly, which befit the Ruler of history (cf. Rom. 11:33), the power and might which enable Him to execute what His wisdom has decreed, and the honor and glory and blessing that shall be His when His right arm has gotten Him the victory.

13-14 There was non in all the created world who could answer the strong angel's challenge and break the malign spell that keeps the world's future a lamentable mystery (cf. 3-4). But since the Lamb has conquered by His dying, none is excluded from His victory; man and man's world will be saved together (cf. Rom. 8:19-21; Col. 1:20). And so it is no wonder that the song of victory is concluded by the cosmic chorus of "every creature" in all creation, who bless and glorify the Enthroned Creator, who made them, and the Lamb, His Servant, who died for the sin that marred them. Their song, with the living creatures' "Amen" and the elders' prostrate devotion which confirms it, binds the vision of Ch. 4 and Ch. 5 together. The church is to know: Though we may rightly distinguish between creation and redemption and confess Creator and Redeemer in distinct articles of our creed, we dare not think or believe them apart from one another. In all the chances and changes of the terrible history which lies between the Now of redemption and the Then of God's "It is done!" (21:6) there is one will at work in which we can wholly trust; whether we pray "Thy Kingdom come" or "Come, Lord Jesus," we are joining in one worship with the living creatures before God's throne, with the 24 crowned and white-robed elders, with the angelic hosts, and with every creature under the sun.

1-2 The Lamb has taken the scroll from the right hand of Him who is seated on the throne, and all creation, angelic, human, and subhuman, has hailed that act as the ultimate triumph of the Lamb's redeeming sacrifice. Now one expects that the hoped-for kingdom of God will come, that the prayed-for triumphal advent of His Christ is at hand. That is "what must soon take place" (1:1). Indeed it must; the visions of Chs. 4 and 5 have assured the hoping and praying church of that. But God's "soon" is other than ours; the events released by the opening of the seals seem to belie her hope and to deny an answer to her prayer: Riders of ruin go forth, four of them, the despairing cry of slain martyrs is heard, and a convulsed and tottering universe seems to cut off forever all human hope for a better day. Things are as they have been; war and dearth and death are rampant as heretofore; indeed, things are to be worse than they have been.

Horse and rider have been from of old a prophetic symbol for powers that patrol the earth to execute God's purposes (cf. Zech. 1:8-10; 6:1-7). The first rider to respond to the living creature's command (nature is in the service of Him who opens the seals): "Come!" sits astride a white horse, resembling in that the victorious Christ as He is portrayed in 19:11; this rider, however, is not the Christ but Antichrist, both imitator and opponent of the Christ. His weapon is not the sword wherewith the Christ shall "smite the nations" (19:15) but the bow, known from Ezekiel (Ezek. 38—39) as the weapon of Gog, the fearsome enemy of God's people in the world's last days (cf. 20:8). By God's consent he wears the victor's crown ("was given to him," passive voice implying divine action) and goes forth "conquering and to conquer." There is a chilling candor in the way the church is matter-of-factly told of Antichrist's coming and of his victory; there lives in this prophecy the same somber sobriety which marks Jesus' words when He makes the coming and the successful lie of false Christs the first sign of His coming. (Matt. 24:4-5)

Some interpreters take the rider on the white horse to be Christ or the victorious Gospel (cf. Mark 13:10) and see in this prophecy an assurance that, in spite of all the hemming disasters which follow, the Gospel will speed and triumph nevertheless. But the resemblance to Gog in the matter of his weapons, the fact that the first rider appears in a series of sinister figures, and the correspondence between the sequence of the signs indicated by the seals and of the signs given by Jesus (Matt. 24:4-8) makes the interpretation given above the more likely one.

3-4 The second rider, astride the bright red horse, corresponds to Jesus' prophecy of "wars and rumors of wars" (Matt. 24:6); "this must take place," Jesus added in the same verse, and His prophet notes that the sword is given to this rider, too, by God: By God's will he will do the dreadful work which shall make all mothers weep and makes peace unknown on earth. The world will grow sick of war ere his work is done, but it will not end war until the new age and its Prince of peace shall end it forever.

5-6 Antichrist and the rider on the red horse are "destroyers of the earth" (11:18). Where they hold sway, the peaceable fruits of the earth cannot flourish. The third rider summoned by the voice of the living creature appears on a horse of ill-omened black and holds in his hand the balances wherewith food is measured out in times of scarcity (cf. Ezek. 4:10; 4:16-17). Food will be dear; a day's work (cf. Matt. 20:2) will, at the inflated price occasioned by dearth, give enough money to buy a man a day's ration of wheat for a man. If he buys the cheaper barley, he may have something for his family, but not much. Necessities will be out of the reach of those who need them; luxuries like oil and wine (cf. Ps. 104:15) will be available for those who can afford them. As usual, the little people will suffer most.

7-8 War and dearth will leave death in their wake. Death rides the fourth, pale, corpse-colored horse, again appearing at the living creature's command. Death is the only winner in this race; Hades, Death's domain, is enlarged behind him as he goes; it "follows" him. As in the case of Antichrist (2) and of the rider astride the red horse of war (4), their triumph is no freakish chance. He who is seated on the throne and the Lamb who opens the seals rule over Death and Hades too; Death and Hades hold their power to destroy because that power is given them, and their power is still limited ("a fourth of the earth"). God's kingdom comes and the authority of the Christ is being established in these chance and varied dyings—

> God moves in a mysterious way
> His wonders to perform,

and the deepest of His mysteries is the mystery of life created through dying, the dying of His Son in order that the dead may live and the dying of His servants in order that they and those who receive their witness may live.

9-10 But the mystery of His way presses hard on the servants of the "Sovereign Lord"; they die, not despite the fact that they are His servants but because they are His servants, who have kept and witnessed to His Word. They see the Antichrist victorious and feel that their history, going its old familiar way of war and dearth and death, has trodden them down into a meaningless death. But the prophetic word assures them that it is no meaningless death that they have died; the life they have given has been a sacrifice acceptable to God (cf. Phil. 2:17; 2 Tim. 4:6), not forgotten nor wasted. They need not cry out to their "Sovereign Lord," to bid Him hallow His name by vindicating them in their unequal struggle against the inhabitants of the earth, the men whose home and horizon is the earth, men without an eye or a hope for anything beyond it and its glories, the successful and superior men who take the cash of the present and let the credit of the future go.

11 Even now, while their lives are poured out in sacrifice at the foot of God's altar (9), the white robe of vindication and victory is theirs and they are bidden to rest in peace until their fellow servants, destined to die victoriously as they have died, shall have been added to their number. God, who numbers the very hairs on their head (Matt. 10:30), has numbered them all, and His numbering must be made complete before the final victory for all God's people can come. The church has no promise that things will get better by and by, but she is assured that her Lord's beatitude on those who are persecuted for righteousness' sake (Matt. 5:10-12) still holds.

12-17 "Once again . . . I will shake the heavens and the earth and the sea and the dry land," the Lord of hosts had said through the prophet Haggai (Hag. 2:6; cf. Heb. 12:26; Rev. 8:5). The earthquake at the opening of the sixth seal signifies that the old order of kings and nations is passing (Hag. 2:21-22), that the end impends, and that significance is underscored by the appearance of signs familiar from the Old Testament as signs of the great day of the Lord (Is. 13:10; 34:4; Ezek. 32:7; Joel 2:10, 30; 3:15; cf. Matt. 24:29). The Lord's long patience, which by premonitory signs and disasters had bidden men repent (cf. 9:20-21), is at an end. Men, great and small, who have presumed upon His longsuffering (cf. Rom. 2:4) are only driven to mad desperation by the sight of the sure, dependable universe now being shaken into huge uncertainty; they attempt to hide themselves from Him whose eye searches everywhere, in dark caves and under the shelter of the enduring hills; they cry for extinction under the collapsing rocks rather than face the wrath of the enthroned Judge whose patience they have despised, the wrath of the Lamb whose redeeming sacrifice (5:9-10) they have refused. On that great day of wrath (cf. Zeph. 1:14-18) the strutting "kings . . . and the great men and the generals and the rich and the strong" will strut no more.

Interlude: The Numbered Saints and the Redeemed Multitude
7:1-17

1 The Lamb has opened six of the seven seals that seal the scroll in God's right hand. There is revealed a succession of terrors, old and new. Antichrist, stirred into action by the triumph of Christ, rides out with a commission of conquest, to deceive and enslave mankind (cf. Ch. 13). The ancient steeds of war, scarcity, and dying harry the world; martyrs cry for vindication and are told that the church's hour of triumph is not yet. And the opening of the sixth seal ushers in a cosmic disintegration which tears to shreds the tent of secular security under which men hide from the eye and arm of God. The latent, silent desperation which gnaws continually at men's hearts becomes open, vocal desperation, and even the most successful of men sense the judgmental visitation of the King and the Lamb. There is wrung from them the desperate cry: "The great day of their wrath has come, and who can stand before it?" (6:17). To that question only God's prophetic word can give answer, and it does give a twofold answer to the church that desires and needs an answer. First, the prophet sees four angels standing at the four corners of the earth restraining the four winds which Jeremiah (Jer. 49:36) had pictured as God's judgmental messengers.

2 The appearance of another angel makes plain the purpose of their restraining action. He comes from a quarter of good omen, that of the rising sun: Paradise lay in the east (Gen. 2:8); there "the sun of righteousness . . . with healing in its wings" will arise (Mal. 4:2); and thence Judaic expectation looked for the coming of the Messiah. **3** This angel's great voice bids the four angels protect man's world until God's servants have been marked upon their foreheads with the seal of God which designates them as God's property, under His protection (cf. Ezek. 9:4, 6). He can protect them, for He is no dumb, impotent idol but the living God.

4 Who are these servants of God? They are the Israel of God on whom His peace and mercy rest (Gal. 6:16): the 12 ancient tribes, but 12 wonderously amplified. The number of the tribes raised to the second power, multiplied by the third power of ten (itself the number of the rounded whole; cf. the ten plagues in Egypt and the Ten Commandments), gives 144,000 as the number of those under God's protection. They, all of them, can face the great day of God's wrath unafraid and can endure all intervening terrors until the day of judgment pronounces them innocent and they are permitted to hear the great invitation, "Come, O blessed of my Father, inherit the kingdom prepared for you from the foundation of the world." (Matt. 25:34)

5-8 The roll of the tribes is called with solemnly monotonous iteration, to make assurance double sure for all the troubled sons of Israel. The tribe of Judah occupies the first place, for Judah is the tribe of the Christ (cf. Heb. 7:14). The tribe of Dan is omitted; from Dan the Antichrist was to come (according to a tradition based on Jer. 8:16), and adherents of the Antichrist have no place among the numbered and protected saints.

9 That is one half of the answer. God has numbered and sealed all His saints. He owns them and will protect them. The other half of the answer is given in the second vision, that of an innumerable host standing before the throne and the Lamb, men of all nations clothed in the pure white robes of vindication and victory, in their hands the palm branches borne by those who kept the Feast of Booths when Israel, the year's work done, gave thanks for the ingathered harvest and recalled the hard but blessed days of her wanderings in the wilderness (Lev. 23:33-43), those days when she lived "in a land not sown" (Jer. 2:2) and the Lord fed her with His own hand. The prophecy of Zechariah which promised that the once-hostile nations should one day join in the celebration of the Feast of Booths (Zech. 8:18-23) will be fulfilled.

10 Those who sing at this last feast of ingathering and homecoming sing a song of victory which gives all glory to God and to the Lamb. "Salvation," victorious deliverance from a desperate situation by the vertical miracle of God's help (cf. Ex. 14:13-14), has no human author (cf. Ps. 3:8). **11** In such a song angels may join; **12** they do worshiping obeisance as they pronounce their assent ("Amen!") and ascribe to Him all that His saving act displays and all the response it evokes.

13-14 Of all the visions recorded in The Revelation to John, only two receive a detailed explanation, the present one of the great white-robed multitude and that of "the judgment of the great harlot" Babylon (17:1-18). The triumph of the apparently defeated servants of God here and the judgment upon the apparently invincible community of the Antichrist there are anything but transparent facts, and the symbols thereof need interpretation. The prophet confesses his inability to interpret the symbol of the great white host when he is questioned by one of the elders of the heavenly court. He needs to be told that these white-robed triumphant men are victors of no ordinary sort. They have come victorious out of the great tribulation foretold by Daniel (Dan. 12:1), a prophecy reiterated by Jesus Himself (Matt. 24:21). This their victorious emergence from martyrdom has been a personal, willed act of sacrifice—"*they* have washed their robes"; but their robes are white and they are victorious not by virtue of their own heroism and deserving but by virtue of Another's blood. They have washed white their robes of victory because there has been, before them and for them, a Victor, the Lamb, whose blood can make the foulest clean. (Cf. 1:5; 5:9)

15 To Him they owe their present victorious purity and their everlastingly assured future. For them Jesus' promise that sons of the resurrection, born into that new age by the resurrection of their Lord (cf. 1:18), shall be "equal to angels" (Luke 20:36) is fulfilled. They stand where angels stand (cf. 8:2), before the throne of God, and they serve Him in His temple. The service to which Jesus' cross has consecrated them (Matt. 20:26-28) will be their eternal privilege; they serve as priests by day and night, forever secure under the tabernacling presence of God the King, who shelters them.

16 His presence will be shelter enough, and food and drink too; the ills which men in the wilderness are heir to (cf. 12:6) will no more be theirs. Hunger and thirst and scorching heat shall not torment this new Israel in the last exodus (cf. Is. 49:10). **17** For the Lamb, the incarnation of God's benignly royal reign, will be their divine Good Shepherd and "will guide them to springs of living water" that never fail (cf. Ps. 23:2; Ezek. 34:23). God Himself, having swallowed up death forever, will wipe away all tears from their eyes. (Is. 25:8)

"Even the hairs of your head are all numbered," Jesus told His apostles (Matt. 10:30); "You are numbered," His prophet tells the apostolic (cf. 21:14) church; "God has numbered and sealed you for His own." Neither Jesus nor John promises the new 12 tribes exemption from the great tribulation that is to come. But just as Jesus promised that "the powers of death shall not *prevail* against" His church (Matt. 16:18), so John holds before the church's eyes the twin vision of her numbered security and of the beatified great white host and grounds the church's hope firmly in the cross of Christ (14). When he reiterates his Lord's "Fear not!" (Matt. 10:26, 28, 31), he speaks with a credible accent.

The Third Vision:
The Seventh Seal and the Seven Trumpets
8:1—11:19

The First Four Trumpets

1 "This must take place, but the end is not yet" (Matt. 24:6), Jesus said when He had spoken of the appearance of false Christs and of "wars and rumors of wars" as signs of His coming and of the close of the age (cf. Matt. 24:3-6). In the message of John, Jesus' servant, there is a similar retardation of the final fulfillment. The opening of the seventh seal does not yet bring on at once the expected close of the age. No "living creature" in the service of God as yet cries, "Come!" (cf. 6:1, 3, 5, 7) to usher in the final stroke of divine judgment and God's ultimate act of deliverance. Instead, there is silence in heaven, while all creation waits for the next action of the Almighty.

2 During that half hour's silence the prophet beholds the seven archangels (Judaic tradition gave them all names; the Bible knows only two angelic names, Gabriel and Michael; cf. Dan. 8:16; 9:21; Luke 1:19, 26; Dan. 12:1; Jude 9; Rev. 12:7). They stand in order serviceable before the God whom they serve (to "stand before" is Old Testament language for to "be in the service of," cf. Dan. 1:5; in other passages the RSV translates the Hebrew phrase "stand before" more freely, e. g., Gen. 41:46; 1 Sam. 16:21; 1 Kings 1:2; Jer. 52:12). To them are given seven trumpets.

For John and his readers the trumpet would be familiar as a military signal (Num. 10:9) and especially as a signal in holy war. John's vision begins with seven trumpets and ends with the fall of a hostile city (11:13) and the disclosure of the ark of the covenant, throne of God the unseen (11:19). Readers would recall the holy war in which Jericho was captured, when the seven trumpets blown by priests laid low the city's walls and escorted the ark of the covenant in the unseen King's triumphal entry (Joshua 6:1-16). Trumpets were blown at the accession of a king (1 Kings 1:34, 39; 2 Kings 9:13), and the sound of the trumpet is heard in psalms which celebrate God's enthronement as King (Ps. 47:5; 98:6).

At the blast of the seventh trumpet in John's vision, loud voices in heaven proclaim the kingship of the "Lord and of his Christ" (11:15, cf. 17). John's trumpet vision is introduced by prayer (8:2-4) and is intended to move men to repentance (9:20-21; cf. 11:13); the Old Testament also associates prayer and the summons to repentance with the sound of the trumpet (e. g., 2 Chron. 13:14; Joel 2:1, 15, cf. 2:12-13). And the Old Testament as well as the New knows of the trumpet as the signal which heralds the great last day of the Lord; the sealed and numbered saints (7:1-8) would know that the events signaled by the trumpeting archangels are last-days actions of God, actions that carry His purposes of judgment and redemption to their victorious close:

> Then the Lord will appear . . .
>   and his arrow go forth like lightning;
> the Lord God will sound the *trumpet*
>   and march forth . . . .
> On that day the Lord their God will save them,
>   for they are the flock of his people;
> for like the jewels of a crown
>   they shall shine on his land.
> (Zech. 9:14, 16; cf. Joel 2:1;
>   Zeph. 1:15-16; Matt. 24:31; 1 Cor. 15:52)

3 Before God's trumpeters begin their solemn task, God arms His servants with a potent weapon of defense: prayer. Another angel (Judaism spoke of an "angel of peace," a mediator between God and man) appears at the altar, where God's justice and mercy meet and are reconciled (cf. Is. 6:6-7). The censer in his hand shows his business is prayer, incense being the accompaniment (Luke 1:10) and the symbol (Ps. 141:2) of prayer. 4 The embattled saints are to know that when they pray, "Thy kingdom come!" the very angels of God assist their prayer with clouds of incense and assure its fragrant ascent to the throne of grace.

5 It *is* a "throne of grace" (Heb. 4:16) for them, however much God's frowning providence may seem to hide His smiling face when fiery judgment showers from His altar amid "peals of thunder, voices, flashes of lightning, and an earthquake" which tell a careless world that God is not mocked. Thus God hallows His name. (Cf. Ezek. 36:22-23)

6 Now, when God's purpose of judgment and grace has been made plain, the trumpeters may blow. **7** At the blast of the first trumpet God vindicates the holiness of His name by visiting the earth with "hail and fire, mixed with blood," a visitation resembling the seventh Egyptian plague, whereby God punished the oppressors of His people and bade them set His people free (Ex. 9:23-25). The phrase "mixed with blood" does not occur in the Exodus account of the seventh plague; it may be an indication that this appeal for repentance will be written in the blood of witnessing martyrs; or it may be taken from Ezekiel's record of the terrors wherewith God threatens Gog and his hordes when they come against the land of Israel: "I will summon every kind of terror against Gog, says the Lord God; every man's sword will be against his brother. With pestilence and *bloodshed* I will enter into judgment with him; and I will rain upon him and his hordes . . . torrential rains and hailstones, fire and brimstone. So I will show my greatness and my holiness and make myself known in the eyes of many nations. Then they will know that I am the Lord" (Ezek. 38:21-23). This judgment, like that of the second, third, and fourth trumpets (8:8-12), is preliminary and partial; it is designed to call men to repentance before the final catastrophe comes and therefore does not strike man directly but only man's world, the old dependable *earth* which nurtures and shelters man with its trees and green grass; and even here the visitation, though more widespread than the earlier visitations at the opening of the sealed scroll, is only partial ("a third" instead of "a fourth," 6:8).

8 At the blast of the second trumpet a great fiery mass "like a great mountain" (Jeremiah used the phrase to describe the destructive power of ancient Babylon, Jer. 51:25) wreaks havoc in the sea. **9** As at the first Egyptian plague (Ex. 7:20-21), the water turns to blood. Man's harvest of the teeming sea (cf. Zeph. 1:3) is shortened by a third, and a third of the ships that ply the sea in search of gain are destroyed. Partial though it be, this visitation is enough to set men "fainting with fear and with foreboding of what is coming on the world" and there will be "distress of nations in perplexity at the roaring of the sea" and its bloodied waves. (Luke 21:25-26)

10 God is Lord of all waters (Job 12:15), and the stars fight for His cause (Judg. 5:20). At the blast of the third trumpet His judgment strikes the fresh waters too. A great star, blazing like a torch in its meteorlike descent, falls on the salubrious rivers and fountains which spell life for man. **11** The name of the star indicates its effect; "wormwood" is a bitter herb (cf. Prov. 5:3-4; Lam. 3:15). The waters made bitter by it bring death to many (though the herb known to men as "wormwood" is not poisonous).

12 One by one, all hopes of a secular security are cut off; earth and sea and living waters offer no security for man when he opposes God (cf. Amos 9:1-4). And as for the sun, moon, and stars set in heaven by the Father of lights (James 1:17) "for signs and for seasons and for days and years" (Gen. 1:14), they, too, fail at the fourth judgmental trumpet blast of God; sun, moon, and stars are stricken. Man is left darkling, in a darkness like that of the terrifying plague which all but moved Pharaoh to let God's people go. (Ex. 10:21-29)

The First and Second Woe:
The Fifth and Sixth Trumpets
8:13—9:21

13 The remaining trumpet blasts are set apart from the first four of the series of seven by the appearance of an angel flying in mid-heaven, where all may see and hear him. With an eagle's strident cry he utters a threefold woe (cf. 9:12; 11:14) upon the inhabitants of the earth, the men "with minds set on earthly things" (Phil. 3:19; cf. Rev. 6:10). What follows at the succeeding three trumpet blasts is thus solemnly marked out as climactic over previous visitations. Now man will be directly struck by demonically uncanny powers. (Ch. 9)

9:1-2 The blast of the fifth trumpet brings on a plague of locusts. A plague of locusts as an instrument of divine judgment and deliverance is familiar to us from the eighth plague on Egypt and from the prophecy of Joel (Ex. 10:12-20; Joel 1:4—2:11). Both ancient and modern descriptions of such a "natural" plague leave no doubt of its devastating terror. But the plague of this vision is no "natural" plague, alignable with other disastrous events and somehow explicable. It comes from no known quarter of the earth. A meteoric figure authorized by God ("was given the key," cf. 1:18) releases the plague from "the bottomless pit," from the dark nether world of evil which God in His mercy usually hides from the sight of man. Now the angel, starlike in his descent, opens it, and from its depth there issues a smoky cloud which darkens the sun and the air.

3-4 From this smoke locusts issue forth. (Our more analytic modern minds would say, perhaps, that on closer view the smoke from the shaft became discernible as a swarm of locusts.) But as these locusts issue from no known quarter, so too they are equipped with no familiar locust power. They have "the power of scorpions," who attack with their agonizing sting man himself, not merely the verdure which feeds man, as locusts ordinarily do. Only those whom God has protected with His seal upon their foreheads can escape this plague.

5 For five months (the ordinary life-span of the locust) these locusts are allowed to torture man. And those five months are the very tortures of hell, **6** a torture from which man cannot be released even by death. In those days men will be like hopeless Job when he cursed the day of his birth and cried:

> Why is light given to him that is in misery,
>   and life to the bitter in soul,
> Who long for death, but it comes not,
>   and dig for it more than for hid treasures;
> Who rejoice exceedingly,
>   and are glad, when they find the grave?
> Why is light given to a man whose way is hid,
>   whom God has hedged in?
> (Job 3:20-23; cf. Jer. 8:3)

Men are desperately "hedged in"; they are not permitted to escape in death. They are condemned to live on and suffer.

7-9 The elaborated description of the locusts, which now follows, makes even more evident their uncannily demonic character. The known locusts provide analogies for their appearance, but this is no description of ordinary vermin, however harmful. The eye of terror with which Joel once beheld a plague of locusts provides some touches for the

71

depiction of these terrible creatures whose onset resembles that of horses caparisoned for battle, who have human faces and heads crowned with gold (why the feminine and lovely feature of "hair like women's hair," suggested by the antennae of the locusts, should prove the ultimate horror is more readily sensed than explained), lions' teeth, "scales like iron breastplates," and wings whose whirr is "like the noise of many chariots . . . rushing into battle."

10 They resemble scorpions in the manner of their sting and locusts in their life-span, 11 but these scorpion-locusts are insects of the nether world, their leader is "the angel of the bottomless pit" from which they have come, and his name is (in Hebrew) Abaddon or (in Greek) Apollyon. Both names mark him as an infernal Destroyer. "Sheol and Abaddon [in the Old Testament a *place* of destruction, here in Revelation personified as an *agent* of destruction] lie open before the Lord" (Prov. 15:11), and He can summon thence agents of whom man does not know and with whom man cannot deal.

12 The eagle crying in midheaven had threatened the inhabitants of the earth with three woes (8:13). The first of the three has been suggested rather than literally depicted in the vision of the locusts from the abyss. There are more to come.

13 When the sixth angel blows his trumpet, a voice is heard issuing from "the golden altar before God." The prayers of the saints had been wafted upward with incense kindled at that altar, and their prayers had issued in judgment upon the world (8:3-6). Their prayer, "Thy kingdom come!" has been answered in a startling way. Through judgment God's mercy finds its way, and so His kingdom comes.

14 The voice from the altar bids the sixth trumpeter release four angels—not now four angels who hold back the tempestuous winds in order that the servants of God may be sealed in peace (cf. 7:1-3) but 15 four angels held ready by God for just this moment of judgment: They await His uses at the river Euphrates, the "great river" which marked the utmost eastern boundary of the Promised Land (Gen. 15:18; Deut. 1:7); thence Isaiah had threatened judgment for his

people (Is. 8:5-8), and thither men of the Roman Empire looked in fearful expectancy for the coming of the mounted Oriental hordes who threatened their security. But it is not from any geographical Euphrates that the visitants shall come whose business is "to kill a third of mankind." **16** No Oriental cavalry was ever mustered in such numbers, 200,000,000 strong. (The prophet's phrase "I heard their number" makes clear that the unbelievable number was a part of his vision, not a figment of his fancy.)

17 Nowhere on earth was ever seen such cavalry before. The riders are mentioned only once and then merely, it would seem, because of the colors of their breastplates, which correspond to the fire, smoke, and sulphur issuing from their horses' mouths. **18** With these hellish plagues (cf. 14:10; 19:20; 21:8), reminiscent of God's judgment on Sodom and Gomorrah (Gen. 19:24, 28), they kill a third of mankind. As in 8:7, 9, 10, 12 destruction is not yet total. By the mercy of God there is still time for repentance, even now when man is left helpless before this infernal cavalry, **19** whose mouths issue gasping destruction and whose tails are wounding serpents. (This twofold head-and-tail attack was probably suggested by the tactics of Rome's dreaded eastern enemies, the Parthians. The Parthian cavalry discharged one volley of arrows as they advanced on the enemy and another volley, over their horses' tails, as they withdrew out of range of their opponents' missiles.)

20 "I smote you . . . yet you did not return to me . . . I overthrew some of you, as when God overthrew Sodom and Gomorrah . . . yet you did not return to me" (Amos 4:9, 11); thus the Lord of hosts once reproached impenitent Israel when He spoke through Amos, and the same reproach must needs be uttered now when God has spoken through trumpet and plague in The Revelation to John. Men do not turn, even when smitten by these visitations, from the gods their own hands have made (cf. Is. 2:8, 20), from the costly futility of manufactured gods who can neither see nor hear nor walk. The wrath of God revealed against the ungodliness of men does not turn them from their ungodliness; for they suppress the manifested truth of God by their wickedness (Rom. 1:18) **21** and will not be diverted from their murders, sorceries, immoralities, and thefts. The basic, root sin of man, his ungodliness, continues to manifest itself in the sins of man, stubbornly and persistently; the mounting intensity of God's judgments evokes from man a mounting intensity of resistance: The judgments of the seals left men merely desperate (6:15-17); the judgments of the trumpets leave them impenitent. They will not turn for healing to the God who has smitten them.

The very exuberance of these wild prophecies of torturing locusts and resistlessly destructive cavalry is a salutary warning against all attempts to trace out "fulfillments" of them in the transparent facts of history. (In World War I there were those who saw in tank warfare a "fulfillment" of Rev. 9:13-19.) These prophecies show us the futility of such attempts: God in His judgmental wooing of man-gone-wrong can work in heights and depths and with means which the transparent facts of history conceal rather than disclose. As long as we confine ourselves to these transparent facts, we can still conceal from ourselves our impotence—and God's omnipotence—with old trite phrases like "Man has always recovered; we'll survive somehow." We can still refuse to face the fact that man is at dead end and that there is only one way to turn, that is, to God in penitent submission, abandoning the idols our hands have made.

Interlude: Assurance for the Prophet
and for the Church
10:1—11:13

Between the sixth and seventh seals there was a pause, an interlude which assured the church of preservation and victory (Ch. 7). Similarly there is a pause between the sixth and the seventh trumpet, and this pause too is an interlude of assurance, assurance both for the prophet (Ch. 10) and for the church. (11:1-13)

The trumpets of God have, apparently, been sounded in vain; the word of prophecy has, apparently, been spoken to no purpose. An unrepenting world continues in its old ways of ungodliness and unrighteousness, and the church sees in history no assurance that her prayers have been set before God as acceptable incense (cf. 8:3-5). Prophet and church are

74

both in danger of lapsing into the apathy of hope deferred.

1 The prophet receives from God Himself the assurance that his message and his office are no vain thing. A "mighty angel" (the second of three angels so named, cf. 5:2 and 18:21) descends from heaven, clad in the cloudy panoply of heaven, with the rainbow of the compassionate God of the covenant over his head (cf. 4:3), with the Son of Man's bright face of victory (cf. 1:16), and with His resistless fiery feet. (Cf. 1:15)

2 His business is revelation; he holds in his hand a scroll. Two things distinguish this scroll from the scroll of 5:1-10. First, this scroll is *not* "sealed with seven seals" (5:1) but "open" (literally, opened). No mighty angel challenges the universe to open the scroll, which only the Lamb that was slain was worthy to open (5:7-9). He who has "ransomed men for God" (5:9) has opened up the Gospel of the royal and priestly future of men. This scroll is freely given to men; the prophet is enjoined to take it and to make it his own (8-9). Second, this scroll is "little"; its content is not the whole mystery of the redemption of the world contained in the great scroll "written within and on the back" (5:1). Rather, as the sequel shows (Ch. 11), this little scroll will reveal the part which the church plays in the drama of redemption, by its dying witness to the Gospel of man's redemption, what Christ's men do by taking up their cross and following Him into death and so into His life (Matt. 16:24-25). In token of his comprehensive authority, the angel bestrides the sea on which Christ's witnessing men will sail and the land on which they will walk. **3** He cries out with a voice that resembles the leonine roar of the Lord, the Judge of all nations (Amos 1:2), and to this roar "the seven thunders" give an answering echo.

4 "*The* seven thunders" would seem to be an allusion to the sevenfold "voice of the Lord" in Ps. 29, which reveals the "glory and strength" (Ps. 29:1) of the Lord in both their terrifying fury (Ps. 29:3-9) and in their assuring and comforting power (Ps. 29:10-11). The allusion to Amos 1:2 in the description of the angel's leonine roar (3) probably indicates that the glory and strength here are the glory and strength of God the Judge of all nations. This explains why "a voice from heaven" imposes restraint upon the prophet when he is about to record what the seven thunders have said. The prophet (as well as the church that hears his word) is reminded that the Lord is Judge, in exclusive sovereignty (cf. Rom. 12:19; Deut. 32:35), as Jesus, His "faithful witness" (1:5), has testified (Matt. 7:1). The prophet in proclaiming the Gospel of "the mystery of God" with which he is entrusted (see comments on v. 7) must needs announce the wrath and judgment of God (cf. 11:17-18); but his commission is to proclaim the Good News, and he is not permitted to become merely a complete expounder (seven!) of God's wrath for its own sake. No prophetic sense of frustration and no suffering which he shares with the church (cf. 11:9) can authorize the prophet to exceed his commission. "No prophecy ever came by the impulse of man" (2 Peter 1:21). Even the inspired prophet proclaims, not everything which he, or God's people, wish to know but all that they need to know.

5-6 What God's people, and above all the prophet himself, now need to know, at this crisis, is told them by the mighty angel; they need to be assured of the validity of the prophetic message concerning "what must soon take place" (1:1). Now men are, naturally enough, asking, "Will it take place? Will it be soon, as we understand 'soon'?" With the upraised hand of one taking oath (cf. Deut. 32:40; Dan. 12:7) the mighty angel swears by the living God who can act when He wills, by the Creator whose illimitable power knows no limitations (cf. Is. 40:12-17, 21-31), that there will be no more delay, that the Lord will not be slow about the fulfillment of His promises, as men may reckon slowness. (2 Peter 3:9)

7 There remains but one more blast of the trumpet before "the mystery of God" will be fulfilled. The living God is "watching over His word to perform it" (Jer. 1:12); He will bring to its full unfolding the "mystery," the plan He has "announced" for the establishment of His royal reign, strange as that plan may seem. The plan seemed strange when the prophet Daniel received the good news of it. (The word rendered "announced" is, literally, "gave the good news to; gospeled.") In Daniel's vision the kingdoms of this world were represented by an image mighty, bright, and frightening, while the kingdom of God was but an unimpressive stone, though a stone "cut out by no human hand"

(Dan. 2:34, 45). What promise was there visible in that stone that it should one day crush and grind to powder the imposing colossus of the kingdoms of this world and become "a great mountain which filled the whole earth" (Dan. 2:35)? What probable promise was there in Daniel's day that the God of a captive people should one day reign supreme and reign alone? (Dan. 2:31-45). What promise was there in Jesus' day, when He took up and proclaimed anew the good news of the mystery (cf. Mark 4:11: "the *secret* of the kingdom"), that the coming of a hedge-preacher from Galilee, on His own description a sower of unpromising seed (Matt. 13:1-9; Mark 4:1-9), was the dawn of the coming kingdom of God? Only eyes opened by God Himself could see that (Matt. 13:11, 16-17). What promise was there, when Paul wrote, that the "secret and hidden wisdom of God" (1 Cor. 2:7; cf. 2:3) manifested in the Crucified should ever be victorious over sin and death (1 Cor. 15:51-57)? What promise was there, in John the prophet's day, when Antichrist rode forth victory-crowned, "conquering and to conquer" (6:2), when martyrs cried for vindication (6:9-11; cf. 2:13) and history threatened to become once more a hell-let-loose (6:1-8), that there would be *soon* "loud voices in heaven saying, 'The kingdom of the world has become the kingdom of our Lord and of his Christ'" (Rev. 11:15)? The prophet, and the church too, needed a voice from heaven to assure them that the prophet's message was a true one and worthy of all acceptation.

8 The prophet is thus assured of the divine validity of his message. He is also assured of the validity of his office, of his prophetic authority to utter his message as the word of God. This assurance is given him in a vision which recalls the commissioning of the prophet Ezekiel (Ezek. 2:8—3:3). The voice from heaven (cf. 4) bids him take the opened scroll from the hand of the angel bestriding sea and land.

9 Accordingly he approaches the angel and demands the scroll from him; the angel bids him eat the little scroll (a homely but telling image to describe inspiration: The word comes to the prophet from without but is assimilated by him and becomes a part of him) and predicts that it will prove bitter food in his stomach though sweet in the mouth at eating. The bitter-sweet experience of eating the scroll is an elaboration of Ezekiel's experience. Ezekiel records merely that when he had eaten the scroll, "it was in my mouth as sweet as honey" (Ezek. 3:3); but he gives a hint that being a spokesman for God is a bitter-sweet experience by noting that the scroll was inscribed with "words of lamentation and mourning and woe" (Ezek. 2:10). The experience promised to John has a complete parallel in the experience of Jeremiah, who says:

> Thy words were found, and I ate them,
> and thy words became to me a joy
> and the delight of my heart (Jer. 15:16).

And then he goes on to describe how being the bearer of God's word shut him out from companionable merriment and left him embittered and solitary (Jer. 15:17). So it will be with John. **10-11** He finds the high privilege sweet to the taste, but he knows that his office will mean that he will be "a torment to those who dwell on the earth" (11:10) and will leave him with a bitter bellyful. John is assured, not that his office will make him "happy" but that it will prove valid and be effective.

11:1 The message of the prophet is validated, and his office has received divine inspiration and sanction (Ch. 10). What of the servants of God, His saints, the church? What may they expect amid the mounting clamor of God's judgmental trumpets and the infatuated impenitence of man? The prophet is inspired to tell the church: There will be and remain forever one holy church; there will be a temple and an altar, the place of God's presence among men which shall give the city of God a right to the name "The Lord is there" (Ezek. 48:35). In terms reminiscent of Ezekiel's vision of the new city and temple of God (Ezek. 40—48) the prophet is told to measure with a measuring rod or reed the place of God's presence, the place of His atoning presence with His worshiping people. The measuring of the church, like the measuring of God's Israel in 7:4-8, indicates that the church has its determined and immovable place in the counsels of God. What He has measured He has claimed as His own and has taken under His protection.

2 Not that "church membership" is an infallible guarantee of preservation. Only those who seek God in His temple and there worship Him and the Lamb have such a guarantee. The outer court of casual and superficial connection with the church is left outside God's protective measurement, and over it shall sweep the harsh vicissitudes of history, where human nations shall trample and desecrate mere man-made sanctities. This will take place during those 42 months (also called 1,260 days; cf. 12:14; Dan. 7:25; 12:7) during which God gives limited license to persecuting powers, in order to try and sift His saints (as He had done in the dark days of Antiochus Epiphanes; from the length of his reign, 3½ years of terror in Jerusalem, 167—164 B.C., the number is derived).

3 During critical days God will not leave Himself without witness. He will give His church the grace and power of prophecy. The church is symbolized by "two witnesses," to identify her closely with "Christ the faithful witness" (1:5) and to mark her as the witnessing martyr-church (cf. 2:13; 6:9; 12:11; 13:10; 16:6; 20:4). The future of the Word of God is the future of the church, both in her suffering and in her victory. As "the word of . . . God will stand forever" (Is. 40:8), so the church is *ecclesia perpetuo mansura* (the church that will endure forever), even as Christ, the Prime Witness, is "alive for evermore." (1:18)

4 The designation of the witnesses as "olive trees" and "lampstands" marks them as the anointed of God, consecrated and empowered by Him for service to Him. This imagery is derived, rather freely, from Zechariah's vision where the two olive trees which stand beside, and provide oil for, the golden seven-branched lampstand are called "the two anointed who stand by the Lord of the whole earth" (Zech. 4:2-14), the reference being to Zerubbabel, the anointed king, and Joshua, the anointed priest. Those who by Christ's sacrifice have been made "a kingdom of priests" (1:5-6) are heirs to the Messianic-priestly promise given to Zerubbabel (Zech. 4:6-10) and to Joshua. (Zech. 3:6-7)

5 This makes the two witnesses inviolable. Whoever would harm them will do so at his peril. Their word, like the prophet Elijah's, could bring down fire to consume their enemies (2 Kings 1:10, 12) **6** and shut the sky and bring on drought (1 Kings 17:1), or like Moses' word turn water into blood (Ex. 7:17-19) or smite the earth with every sort of plague at will. (1 Sam. 4:8)

7 The two witnesses will complete their testimony, no matter what may oppose or seek to destroy them; when the Word of the Lord shall have been fully spoken, there will be a last, climactic attack upon them. From "the bottomless pit," whence the fearful plague of locusts had arisen at the sounding of the fifth trumpet (9:1-3), "the beast" (identified as Antichrist in 13:1-10) will arise to make war upon those whose voices, with their "No!" to all the bestial greatness of man, have so long been a torment to mankind. His attack will be successful; the beast will conquer and kill them. The witnesses will, like their Lord before them, not only be killed but also be degraded in death, their bodies left unburied. (Cf. Jer. 22:18-19)

8 The two witnesses will share the fate of their Lord, "the faithful witness" (1:5), killed and degraded in the "great city" which may claim to be the holy city but is, to eyes opened by the Spirit (cf. footnote *d* and Eph. 1:17-18), as degenerate and impious as Sodom and a greater oppressor of God's people than Egypt ever was. In that great city, whose prime characteristic is that its citizens unite to speak their "No!" to God's grace, as once Gentile and Jew united to crucify the Lord in Jerusalem, there the two witnesses will glorify their Lord by accepting freely the shame of a death like His.

9 For "three days and a half"—the 3½ years of judgment upon the pseudochurch (2) has its counterpart in the 3½ days of the defeat of the witnessing church—men of all nations gaze with vindictive satisfaction on the defeated and unburied witnesses. The presence here of this multinational and polyglot multitude is another indication that "the great city . . . where their Lord was crucified" (8) is not to be taken in any literal historical-geographical sense of Jerusalem in Palestine. "The great city" (16:19; 17:18; 18:10, 16, 18, 19, 21) is not even, precisely and flatly, Rome either, the persecuting power which confronted John and his first readers. It is a symbol for every and any place where men "spurn the Son of God and profane the blood of the covenant by which they were sanctified and outrage the Spirit of grace" (Heb. 10:29). It is a symbol of all "religious" opposition to the true God, whose reality as the God "who lives forever" (10:6) is the haunting question mark placed before all false gods and all pseudoreligion.

10 The death of the two witnesses will be the occasion of rejoicing and merriment (cf. John 16:20); there will be a festival, a sort of anti-Christmas, at which men exchange presents, probably choice portions from the festal meals (Esther 9:19, 22). The torment of the prophetic presence is over, and the men of the great city breathe more easily again.

11 "Dying, and behold we live" (2 Cor. 6:9). The festive triumph of those who have silenced the two witnesses of God is short-lived. As the Spirit of God had once, in Ezekiel's vision, brought life into the dead, bleached bones of Israel, captive and desolate, and there was a rattling as bones came together, bone to its bone, and the bones were covered with sinews and flesh and were clothed with skin, and breath came into the dead men of Israel and they stood up (Ezek. 37:1-14), so now these liquidated witnesses of God rise reanimated from their assured death and stand upon their feet. They have followed their crucified Lord into death and into a life which death cannot destroy (cf. Rom. 6:9), to the terror of their enemies.

12 The whole glory of their Lord becomes theirs, His death in service to man, His resurrection, and His ascension. A voice from heaven bids them ascend, and in the sight of the men who have just celebrated their death they go up to heaven as their Lord went "in a cloud." (Cf. Acts 1:9)

13 In that last hour God attests the witnesses who have been faithful unto death with a great final earthquake, an earthquake which decimates the hostile city and brings death to "seven thousand people"—perhaps these doomed 7,000 are the negative counterpart to the faithful remnant of discouraged Elijah's day, the 7,000 who had not bowed the knee to Baal (1 Kings 19:18). Then only 7,000, by the grace of God, survived; now, by the grace of God, only 7,000 are to perish. Here John notices what has not been touched on in the visions of judgment (seals and trumpets, Chs. 6, 8, 9). Here, in this vision of comfort and assurance, he notes that there will be exceptions to the general impenitence of men

81

described in 9:20-21. There will be those who, though unmoved by God's judgments, will be moved by the witness of the martyr-church. They will be filled with terror (or, perhaps better, "with awe") and give "glory to the God of heaven." That is, they will confess their wrong (cf. Joshua 7:6; Luke 18:13) and repent; forgiven, they will be saved, plucked like brands out of the burning. (For the close connection between fear, doing homage, and repentance in Revelation, cf. 14:7; 15:4; 16:9.)

The Third Woe: The Seventh Trumpet
11:14-19

14 Now at last (cf. 8:13; 9:12) "the second woe" is concluded and the final trumpet is to be sounded; now "the mystery of God . . . shall be fulfilled" (10:7) and "the third woe is soon to come." If God's "mystery" were stern legal logic, one might expect the Last Judgment to follow.

15 But though judgment is the end of God's way with the world, it is not the goal of His way. His goal is that He may reign in all the glory of the grace which His Christ has revealed. Therefore the sounding of the seventh trumpet does not yet usher in the Last Judgment. There are to follow further visions which make clear, ere judgment (20:11-15) comes, the ultimate seriousness of the struggle which must take place before all satanic and human opposition to God's reign is overcome and God and His Christ alone shall reign. What we are to witness now, at the sounding of the seventh trumpet, embodies the high confidence of the prophet and the church, the confidence of faith assured and confirmed (Chs. 10—11), in the final victory of the Lord and His Christ. In heaven loud voices (of which the song of the church is the earthly counterpart) already hail that victory as an accomplished fact: The reign of God and His Anointed has been established, the long-prayed-for kingdom has come and shall endure forever and ever.

16 The song of triumph is taken up by the 24 elders, the voice of the church triumphant. **17** They give thanks that God has heard the cry of His saints (cf. 6:10; 8:1-5) and has manifested Himself in His answer as the Lord God Almighty now, as He has in the past; they no longer speak of Him as the

God "who is to come" (cf. 1:4, 8; 4:8); for the adoring faith of the church, since "faith is the assurance of things hoped for" (Heb. 11:1), He *has* come. **18** Faith can look back upon the raging opposition of the powers that conspire against the Christ (Ps. 2:1), an opposition still to be revealed in all its depth in Revelation, as upon a trouble overpast; faith can already hear the derisive laughter of God who, in spite of all the fury of His enemies, has set His anointed King upon His holy hill (Ps. 2:4-9; cf. Rev. 14:1), whose wrath has cleared away the opposition and will deal destructively with the satanic rearguard action of those powers who refuse to worship the Creator (cf. 14:7) but are bent on destroying the earth which He created and called very good (Gen. 1:31). Of those destructive powers preceding visions have already told us much, and succeeding visions will tell us more.

19 God's concluding manifestation of Himself corresponds to the song of the elders. His wrath has come, and the missiles of His armory (cf., e. g., Ps. 18:12-14; Job 38:22-23) advertise its destructive omnipotence. But the eyes of faith may look into God's opened temple and behold there what only the high priest might approach once a year in the olden days, on the Day of Atonement, the ark of the covenant, throne of the unseen King "who keeps covenant and steadfast love" (Deut. 7:9). On this ultimate Day of Atonement all may behold the throne of Him whose forgiving words and redeeming acts have always kept His covenant promise: "I will be your God."

The Last Four Visions:
Christ and the Powers of Darkness
12:1—22:5

In one sense the seven letters (Chs. 1—3), the seven seals (Chs. 4—7), and the seven trumpets (Chs. 8—11) have told the whole of "what must soon take place" (1:1). The church's struggle amid the tribulations that attend the coming of God's kingdom, her apparent defeat, her "patient endurance" in that struggle (1:9), and her ultimate triumph over all opposition have been, in one sense, adequately portrayed. But in another sense the struggle and the triumph have not been portrayed in their full dimensions, nor has the source of the church's enduring strength and of the certainty of her triumph been fully revealed. The source of the church's assurance of victory has, of course, been announced: the crucified and risen redeeming Lord (1:5-6, 17-18; 5:9-10). And there have, to be sure, been glimpses of the dark satanic depths which underly the surface operations of opposition and persecution with which the church must deal: The synagog at Smyrna which slanders the church and threatens her with suffering, imprisonment, and death has been prophetically branded as "a synagogue of Satan" (2:9-10; cf. 3:9); the pretentious paganism of Pergamum has been marked as "Satan's throne" (2:13); the maunderings of the prophetess at Thyatira have been exposed as "the deep things of Satan" (2:24). The plague of locusts at the fifth trumpet blast is seen to be an infernally abysmal visitation; the hellish Destroyer is king over these locusts (9:11). The provenance of the beast who wars upon God's two witnesses is "the bottomless pit." (11:7)

Yet these hints of satanic power at work are but the rolling echoes of the noise of that irreconcilable conflict between God and Satan, between God's kingdom and the satanic counterkingdom, which is the subject of the last four visions. Here we behold the enemy of God, always God's imitative "ape" (Luther), constituting himself as a counter-

Trinity (dragon, first beast, second beast, Chs. 12—13), with a counterchurch to embody his cause on earth (Babylon, Chs. 17—19). The church of God is to know that in her conflict she wrestles not with powers of "flesh and blood" but against "spiritual hosts of wickedness in the heavenly places" (Eph. 6:12) and that her final triumph is no earthly triumph to be won by mundane means of stratagem or compromise but is the ultimate divine triumph divinely won whereby the kingdom of God and the authority of His Christ are forever and universally established. This triumph issues in the Last Judgment (20:11-15) and in the glory of God's new-created world (21:1—22:5). That ultimate judgment is anticipated in the penultimate visitation of the seven bowls of wrath (Chs. 15—16); and the ultimate triumph is anticipated in the triumphal songs of those "who follow the Lamb wherever he goes" (14:4), into death and into His victory over the Antichrist (15:2), and thus into the presence of the manifested glory of the covenant God (15:5-8). Both the judgment (20:4) and the triumph (20:6) are proclaimed as realities already present for "those . . . beheaded for their testimony to Jesus" (20:4) in the vision of the 1,000-year reign of those risen in "the first resurrection." (20:4-6)

The Fourth Vision:
The Attack of the Anti-Trinity
and the Advancing Triumph of Christ
12:1—14:20

The Woman, the Child, and the Dragon
12:1-6

1 The first set of visions (1:9—11:19), depicting the church of Christ in its struggle with the powers of this world, began with the death and resurrection of Christ (1:5; 1:17-18). The second set of visions, depicting the same struggle at a deeper level as the conflict between God and Christ and the satanic powers underlying the powers of this world, goes back to the first stage of the final struggle between God and Satan, to the birth of the Son of God, who "appeared . . . to destroy the works of the devil" (1 John 3:8). The prophet beholds "a great portent . . . in heaven," a sign betokening God's presence and purpose among men, like the signs with

85

which the Lord at the Exodus hardened Pharaoh's heart and set His people free (Ex. 7:3-5), like those wondrous signs whereby God attested His Son Jesus to the men of Israel (Acts 2:22; cf. Matt. 12:28). The sign is "a woman clothed with the sun, with the moon under her feet, and on her head a crown of twelve stars." But for all the splendor of her insignia, she is no vague goddess-figure such as inhabited the imagination of men of many lands, who dreamt of the birth of a savior-child who would bring again the world's golden age. John's readers in the churches of Asia would be familiar with the portrayal of God's people as a woman and mother from their hearing of the Old Testament prophets (cf. Hos. 1—3; Is. 1:8; 54:1; 62:4-5; Jer. 4:30-31), and the 12 stars of her crown would identify her for them unmistakably as Israel of the 12 tribes (12 and multiples of 12 being regularly used to indicate the people of God, 7:3-8; 14:1; 21:12), the mother from whom the Christ came (cf. Rom. 9:4-5). The Christmas story is here being told in a way quite different from the familiar one in the first two chapters of Luke, but in both stories "salvation is from the Jews" (John 4:22). The glory which belongs to the sun-clad, moon-bestriding, star-decked mother is all from above, from the world of God, and stands in sharp contrast to the rich and gaudy decking-out of the harlot Babylon, whose ornaments all come from below, from the earth and the sea. (17:4)

2 This woman's glory, given her by God, is that she is to be the mother of the Messiah, and she has that glory amid agony; she cries out in the anguish of travail (cf. Micah 4:10; 5:3). The inglorious history of Israel, with its unpromising conclusion, as sketched by Matthew in his account of the genealogy of Jesus (Matt. 1:1-17), the fact that Jesus was born to Nazarene parents in Bethlehem, "little . . . among the clans of Judah" (Micah 5:2), because an alien pagan power ruled over Israel (Luke 2:1-5), and the fact that the Messiah's birth occasioned the weeping of mothers in Bethlehem (Matt. 2:16-18) illustrate that anguish.

3 The kingdom of God and the counterkingdom of Satan confront each other from the beginning. The portent of the birth of the Messianic Child has as its counterpart the portent of the gigantic red dragon (ancient and widespread

symbol for the power which opposes God), enemy and would-be destroyer of the Child. The dragon of the portent is a formidable figure; his power is symbolized by his ten horns (ten being the number of the rounded-out whole); his seven diadems (seven being the number of completeness) indicate that the satanic power becomes incarnate in many royal potentates. 4 The dragon's power lashes out at God; his tail even sweeps a third of God's duteous stars from heaven and casts them upon the earth. (Cf. Dan. 8:10)

But his enmity is directed chiefly against the woman and her destined Child. 5 The Child will be the Anointed King who shall with His rod of iron subdue and destroy all that makes the kingdom of this world Satan's kingdom; the kingdom of this world shall be Satan's no more (11:15; cf. Luke 4:5-6). If Satan would endure and reign, he must devour the Child. No compromise is possible. The almost nonchalant sparseness of the record of the triumph of Michael and his angels over the satanic host is itself a witness to the vanity anf futility of the satanic attack: The "child was caught up to God." In those few words the sure certainty of God's triumphant power finds expression, that divine power which carried the Son through His trials (cf. Luke 22:28), His Passion, and His death to His resurrection and gave Him freely the kingdom which He had refused to gain by compromise (Luke 4:5-8) and seated Him at God's right hand (cf. 3:21). One is reminded of the composure with which Jesus awaited the final onslaught of the Enemy on the eve of His Passion: "The ruler of this world [Satan] is coming. He has no power over me" (John 14:30). It is natural to think of Jesus' Passion, for in this story of the birth of the Messiah the story of His Passion and victory is compendiously included; the day of the "birth" of the Anointed King is the day on which He becomes King, the day on which God declares: "You are my son, today I have begotten you" (Ps. 2:7). The day on which Jesus wore His crown of thorns was the day of His enthronement. (Cf. Acts 2:36)

6 The Child is now at the Son's destined place, that seat at God's right hand to which He confidently looked (since the Scriptures promised it to Him) in the days when His questioning enemies were pressing in on Him and death was

imminent (Matt. 22:15-44). His mother, the people of God from whom He sprang, is still on earth, in the wilderness far from her true and lasting home, as Israel once was in the wilderness, far from her Promised Land. But even there God cares for her by providing a place for her and providing food for her as He provided manna and quail for Israel in the wilderness. ("It was I who knew you in the wilderness," Hos. 13:5.) And God sets limits to her time of tribulation; for the 1,260 days, or 42 months, or 3½ years as the period of affliction, see comments on 11:2. With that brief notice of God's protective and preserving care for His people the story of the woman is broken off; it will be resumed in 12:13-17.

The Dragon Is Defeated
12:7-12

7 At the beginning of His ministry Jesus told Nathanael, now led to see in the Man from Nazareth whom he viewed so skeptically (John 1:46) "the Son of God . . . the King of Israel" (John 1:49), that he would "see heaven opened and the angels of God ascending and descending upon the Son of man" (John 1:51). The assault of Satan upon the helpless Messianic Child (12:1-6) is accordingly depicted once more, now as an assault upon the angelic armies of heaven themselves. Michael the archangel, the great prince of God's chosen people (Dan. 10:13, 21), leads God's angelic armies in the battle against the idiot-fury of Satan and satanic angels that would destroy the King of God's chosen people. 8 Their attempt is doomed to failure. "They were defeated," is the prophet's laconic account of the battle, and he adds the nature and the inner significance of their defeat in the words, "There was no longer any place for them in heaven."

9 The dragon and his angels have no place in heaven anymore, for the dragon has been "thrown down." The prophecy uttered by Jesus concerning the effect of His death is fulfilled: "Now is the judgment of this world, now shall the ruler of this world be cast out" (John 12:31). The "ancient serpent" who first misled man (Gen. 3) and so gained his place and power as the accuser of mankind before the throne of God (Satan's power is grounded on the guilt of man, cf.

88

Zech. 3:1-4), he who has hitherto had the power to deceive the whole world with his alluring lies, has lost his place and power.

10 In heaven, in the world of God and His transfigured saints, the victory is fully known and realized; there a loud voice (whether the voice of an angel or of the conquering martyrs, cf. 6:10, is not clear) proclaims the fact and the significance of the divine victory: "Now"—now that the deceiver and accuser has met One whose humanly pure heart he could not deceive, the wholly obedient Son whom he cannot accuse, the Lamb of God who by His dying has taken away the guilt of the world (John 1:29) and has removed all grounds for accusation against mankind—now the sluice gates are opened wide and the waters of mercy pour forth freely, now God's royal mercy can appear in manifested majesty and the authority of His Christ, no longer hidden by His servant's form, is the revealed authority of Him into whose pierced hands the Father has committed all that is in heaven and on earth (Matt. 28:18). For the voice of the accuser has been forever silenced. **11** Now—let the perishing martyr-church give ear—now man's dying is not death but victory, for the redeeming blood of the victorious Lamb (5:12-13) has been shed for all, and men who loved their Lord too well to forbear witnessing to Him even in the face of death may learn the full truth of His word, "Whosoever loses his life for my sake and the gospel's will save it." (Mark 8:35)

12 In heaven, for whose dwellers all joy is present and all sorrow overpassed, may be heard the ultimate echo of Isaiah's exultant cry:

> Sing, O heavens, for the Lord has done it
> (Is. 44:23; cf. 44:22).

But how shall the earth respond to the summons of Isaiah?

> Shout, O depths of the earth;
> break forth into singing, O mountains,
> O forest, and every tree in it. (Is. 44:23)

The great question of man's guilt has been answered; but the lesser question of the devil's remaining power has not, and his descent from heaven bodes ill for land and sea, the abode of man. The time is near when the devil's power, too, will be annihilated (20:10); he knows that, with satanic clairvoyance, and the shortness of the time for his rearguard action only intensifies his fury. How shall the embattled church endure that rage?

The Dragon Pursues the Woman
12:13-17

13 "Be sober, be watchful. Your adversary the devil prowls around like a roaring lion, seeking someone to devour. Resist him, *firm in your faith*," Peter wrote to troubled churches in Asia Minor in his day (1 Peter 5:8-9). The 12th chapter of The Revelation to John speaks the same word to the churches in a visionary, symbolic way. The churches can be firm in their faith, for faith is "the conviction of things not seen" (Heb. 11:1). The eyes of faith can look heavenward and see there the failure of the dragon's assault upon the Messianic Child, the Child enthroned victoriously at God's right hand: They can see the accuser of men cast out from his high place before the throne of God and can behold the church provided for and secure, albeit in "the wilderness" (14). But the eyes of the church are not the eyes of one bemused by dream and delusion; they look with sober vigilance upon the actual present of the church and can see the church imperiled by the fury of the dragon exploiting his still-remaining "short time" (12) in pursuing the woman who is both the mother of the Christ and of all who are His (cf. "the rest of her offspring," 17; Gal. 4:26). The church lives simultaneously in the high confidence of faith and in the open-eyed sobriety of fear.

14 God protected His ancient people amid the perils of the first exodus, and He preserves His new people now in this last exodus. Then He told His people: "You have seen what I did to the Egyptians, and how I bore you on *eagles' wings* and brought you to myself" (Ex. 19:4; cf. Deut. 32:10-12). Those same wings now enable the woman to escape from "the serpent" (cf. 9) into the wilderness, and the ancient love of the Lord of which Hosea spoke,

I am the Lord your God from the land of Egypt . . .
It was I who knew you in the wilderness (Hos. 13:4-5),

that love provides for the new Israel now, during these last wilderness years "for a time, and times, and half a time" (still another way of expressing the 3½ years, or 42 months, or 1,260 days of affliction, Dan. 7:25; Rev. 11:2-3; 12:6; 13:5). What the sealing of the servants of God said in 7:1-8, the escape on eagles' wings from the attacking serpent says here. It speaks assurance:

> Though devils all the world should fill,
> All eager to devour us,
> We tremble not, we fear no ill,
> They shall not overpower us.
> This world's prince may still
> Scowl fierce as he will,
> He can harm us none,
> He's judged; the deed is done . . . .

15 The Lord once saved His people from the peril of whelming waters and led them dryshod to safety (Ex. 14:21-31) in spite of the pursuit of the enemy; so now when the serpent would sweep the woman away with a flood which he spewed forth from his mouth (the symbol may point to the flood of lies with which Satan emperils, and seeks to destroy, the church). **16** The earth which God once blessed and will bless again, the earth destined by Him to be, at the coming of His Messiah,

> full of the knowledge of the Lord
> as the waters cover the sea (Is. 11:9),

God's good earth, from which all hurt and destruction shall be removed (Is. 11:9), comes to the woman's aid and swallows up the river sent to destroy her.

17 The prophet John is not minimizing the threat to the church; he is facing it and describing it realistically. The satanic threat is no bagatelle, nor will it be merely momentary; Satan's fury has shifted from the Child to the mother of the Child; and, foiled in both cases, it now shifts, undiminished, to "the rest of her offspring." Since John portrays the church, the people of God, as *both* inviolable and as under satanic attack, he employs two images to portray her condition: The church as inviolable is imaged in the woman kept secure in the wilderness; the church as under persistent satanic attack is pictured by "the rest of her offspring," as those whom Christ is not ashamed to call His brethren (Heb. 2:11-12), those who "suffer with him" in order that they "may also be glorified with him" (Rom. 8:17). They suffer with Him because they, like Him, are minded to live "by every word that proceeds from the mouth of God" (Matt. 4:4) and because they testify in word and deed and dying to Him who in life and death was a "faithful witness" to the love of God (1:5). To attack them Satan stands poised on the sand of the sea. (Cf. comments on 13:11)

The Beast from the Sea
13:1-10

1 The great dragon, Satan, is the crafty imitator of God. His subordination to God, the enthroned Ruler of all (Ch. 4), the fact that he must remain "God's devil" (as Luther called him), becomes clear in the fact that he works along lines laid down by God and frames his countermelody to sound half a beat behind the music of God. Since God is revealed in a Trinity of Persons (cf. 1:4-5), Satan manifests himself in an antitrinity of dragon (Ch. 12), first beast (13:1-10), and second beast (13:11-18), corresponding to and opposing Father, Son, and Holy Spirit. The satanic antitrinity is marked from the first as a sorry and perverted imitation of the divine Trinity. The prophet sees the Antichrist as "a *beast* rising out of the sea." He comes not to serve and to give himself as a ransom for many (Matt. 20:28). His is the will of the beast of prey which ruthlessly seeks its own. For all his assumed similarity to the divine, he belongs to the low order of those who become great by diminishing others, those who "lord it *over*" and "exercise authority *over*" others in order to become great (Matt. 20:25). Moreover, he rises out of the sea, that element which in the Biblical view is a remnant of subdued chaos forever threatening to become chaos again.

It was from the turbulent sea that Daniel in his vision had seen emerge the four beasts that symbolized the world powers in their enmity and opposition to God's people, "the saints of the Most High" (Dan. 7). Like them, this beast is an impressive entity, with his ten horns of power regally diademed and his seven heads. Looking westward over the sea, John was looking toward Rome; he would be reminded of the power of the Roman Empire and of the massively articulated strength of its imperial organization. The "blasphemous name" on the heads of the beast would recall the titles with which Roman patriotic and religious fervor celebrated its deified emperors: "holy," "eternal," "invincible," "Lord and God," titles blasphemously expressing man's resolve to heed the serpent's voice and to "be like God." (Gen. 3:5)

2 The characteristic features of the beast (leopard, ox, lion) are combined from the several characteristics of the four beasts in the vision of Daniel (Dan. 7). Whatever examples of bestial magnificence the world may have beheld in imperial power before, all appear concentrated in this beast to whom the dragon had given anti-Messianic power, royalty, and great authority.

3 Most wondrous of all, the Antichrist resembles the Lamb that was slain (cf. 5:6)—the Antichrist is also a pseudo-Christ. Alive, he bears upon one of his heads the marks of a mortal wound. No wonder that the whole world follows him with awed veneration. What higher proof of power is there than this? Whose reign can promise life to his subjects more patently than his? **4** "Men worshiped the dragon" who had given such life-giving authority to the Messianic beast; "they worshiped the beast" with the same cry of astonished veneration as that wherewith redeemed Israel once praised the Lord who had triumphed gloriously in setting His people free from Egypt:

> Who is like thee, O Lord, among the gods? . . .
> Thou hast led in thy steadfast love the people
>   whom thou hast redeemed . . . .
> The Lord will reign for ever and ever.
> (Ex. 15:11, 13, 18)

The idea of the Antichrist as a mortally wounded beast who survived death very probably alludes to the mystery surrounding the death of the emperor Nero A. D. 68. No emperor had so insisted on his own deity as he and none had been so "beastly" in his lust and cruelty; the carnival atmosphere with which he surrounded his killing of Christians A. D. 64 sickened his subjects, and even Tacitus, the Roman historian who recorded it years later, does not conceal his disgust. He probably died by his own hand; but there were persistent rumors that, though he had been secretly murdered, he had been snatched away to the East and would return at the head of an Oriental army (the Parthians, dreaded eastern enemy of Rome) to claim his own. Pretenders claiming to be Nero returned to life, one as recently as A. D. 89, some six years before John wrote; a Greek author of the early second century recorded that "most men believe that Nero is still alive."

To the beast belong the world and the future—who but a fool or a madman or those strange creatures, the Christians, would think of resisting him? **5** Yet the Christians, by the power given them through the prophet's vision and voice, can and must resist him (cf. 10). They know how false is the aura of invincibility which surrounds the first beast. They know that in this satanic triumph God is still in control; four times in three verses (5-7) the prophet declares that whatever power the beast has and exercises "was given" him by God and that he does what he does because he "was allowed" by God to do so. And God, the prophet declares, not the dragon and not his Messianic beast, determines the length of Antichrist's reign and the span of his triumph (described with the by-now familiar designation for the time of tribulation, "forty-two months," cf. comments on 11:2). The Antichrist's reign is limited; God and the Lamb shall have "honor and glory and might for ever." (5:13)

6 The Antichrist is not autonomous even in his blaspheming; though he utters great words to bring contempt upon God and His revelation of Himself (His "name") and upon His indwelling presence among men whose "commonwealth is in heaven" (Phil. 3:20), he can do so only because he is "allowed" (5)—the passive voice indicates that it is God who thus allows him— **7** to assail God and His saints in word and deed. He is allowed to "sift" the saints "like wheat" (Luke 22:31) in a war of conquest against them. The saints are subjected also to the fearful pressure of a majority against them (cf. Matt. 7:13-14), for the beast is given authority "over every tribe and people and tongue and nation."

8 The worship of the beast becomes a world religion,

claiming the loyalty of "all who dwell on earth" (cf. 11:10)—except the loyalty of those whom God's elective love has eternally enrolled among the citizens of His eternal city, inscribed in the book of the Lamb whose blood has freed them from their sins and marked them for a home with God as His priests and kings (1:5-6). The pen of God is mightier than the bestial sword.

9 If the saints would live, live in that triumph which Paul describes as "dying, and behold we live" (2 Cor. 6:9), these are the words which they must hear and keep. **10** They must dare to be taken captive; they dare not dare to kill. Their Lord has taken the sword of vengeful slaughter from their hands (cf. Matt. 26:51-52). There is no way to life except His way of faithfulness unto death (2:10). The road into the kingdom runs through dying. The kingdom which Jesus gave to the poor and the persecuted (Matt. 5:3, 10) calls for "endurance and faith," not for the zelotic faith which reaches for the sword.—The cry which challenges the saints to endure and die echoes the language of Jer. 15:2:

> Those who are for pestilence, to pestilence,
> and those who are for the sword, to the sword
> (cf. Jer. 43:11).

An ancient manuscript of Revelation suggests a reading which is an even distincter echo of Jeremiah; this and the fact that it is a more difficult reading and therefore more liable to be modified by ancient copyists (in imitation of Jesus' word, Matt. 26:52) makes it worthy of consideration. We might then read:

> If any one is to be taken captive,
> to captivity he goes;
> If any one is *to be slain* with the sword,
> with the sword must he be slain.

The Beast from the Earth
13:11-18

11 When the prophet looked seaward (12:17; 13:1), he looked toward Rome and was confronted by the power of the Roman Empire, represented by the proconsul, the governor who came annually from Rome. When he faced landward, he looked toward the Roman province of Asia, where the cult of

95

the deified emperor had been welcomed early and enthusiastically, long before it became officially established in Rome itself. In Asia the emperor cult continued to have its most ardent devotees and propagandists, and there the collision between "Lord Caesar" and the Lord Jesus first took place. There men were confronted by the Roman Empire not only in its power but also in its religious hold on men, its fascination for them. The men of varied race, language, and culture who made up the Roman Empire were impressed and subdued by Rome's power (cf. Acts 19:37-40); but it was the religious hold of Rome, particularly that of the emperor cult, which made them willing servants of Rome and enlisted their wills into her service. This religious hold over men Rome recognized and exploited; the cult of the emperor provided an inner bond of cohesion which the polyglot empire lacked and needed. As the Holy Spirit makes men able and willing to call Jesus Lord (1 Cor. 12:3) and to put all their gifts and graces into the service of His lordship (1 Cor. 12:5), so the dragon must needs have his anti-Spirit to make men willing and ardent subjects of his Antichrist. That is the function and office of the second beast, the pseudo-Paraclete who rises from the earth.

He is earthborn and cannot really deny his origin: "He who is of the earth belongs to the earth, and of the earth he speaks" (John 3:31); even though his appearance is an imitation of the Lamb's, his speech betrays him. His origin is not only earthy but satanic. His voice is satanic, **12** and his will is satanic; he turns men inwardly from God and the Lamb toward the dragon and the first beast. He "exercises" (that is, enforces or actualizes, by producing inner conviction) the satanic authority of the first beast "in its presence," that is, on the first beast's authority and at his command; one thinks of the cooperation between the representatives of the emperor cult and the representatives of Roman political power. This elicits from men, not only wondering obeisance (cf. 4) but a worship comparable to the devotion of men to the Lamb—is not the beast "whose mortal wound was healed" comparable (in the minds of men deluded by the second beast's satanic lie) to Him who says, "I died, and behold I am alive"? (1:18)

13 "Signs" such as those which divinely attested Jesus as Christ and Lord (Acts 2:22) satanically attest the Antichrist, signs fatally similar to those which attested the two preachers of repentance as true reincarnations of the prophetic authority of Elijah (11:5). **14** Men whose hearts are not held steady by God's elective love (8) are allowed to be deceived by these signs and to give their hearts to the beast; they are led to make an image in his honor. It was at the image of the emperor (Domitian set up his image everywhere) that fidelity was tested. Men set free by Christ (1:5) could not and would not offer incense at that image as an expression of their allegiance to the deified emperor. For the critical significance of the "image," cf. 14:9, 11; 15:2; 16:2; 19:20; 20:4.

15 God's severest judgment on men who reject His manifested truth and, instead, desire the lie is that He gives them what they desire, with all its fearful consequences (cf. Rom. 1:20-32); He permits the anti-Spirit to give life and speech to the image of the Antichrist, with the result that blindly enraptured devotees of the beast are ready to kill all those who will not join them in their worship of the beast. The image of the beast, "nothing" in itself, becomes alive and terribly effectual for those who worship it (cf. 1 Cor. 10:19-20). **16** All men, whatever their station or standing, who will not have for their protection "the seal of the living God" (7:2) are moved by the anti-Spirit to accept, instead, the mark of the beast on hand or brow, in token that they have become the property of the beast who claims them.

17 The claim of the beast will be enforced by rigorous economic sanctions. The word translated "mark" is found in ancient records as the technical term for the stamp of the emperor (containing his name and the year of his reign) imprinted on deeds of sale and other commercial documents; the term is used also of the "likeness and inscription" (Mark 12:16) of the emperor on Roman coins. Both indicate how deeply and pervasively the conflict between loyalty to Lord Caesar and to the Lord Jesus entered into the ordinary business of living. The churches of Asia are to know: The claim of the deified emperor is not one they can evade or come to terms with. The beast's mark and number (cf. 18) states a totalitarian claim and states it both comprehensively and brutally.

18 How are the churches to recognize that name and number? This calls for wisdom, insight into God's mysterious ways, and the God who gives wisdom to men under trial when they ask for it in faith (James 1:5-6) will give them wisdom. The number is a human number and therefore decipherable in human history by human minds. The number 666 (some ancient authorities read 616) indicates, though it does not explicitly state, the name. In both Hebrew and Greek, letters of the alphabet were used for numbers, instead of numerals. By substituting the numerical value of each letter of a noun (e. g., one-two-two-one, or 1221, for "abba") one could produce a cryptogram of the noun, readily decipherable to those in the know. But since the numerical value could be arrived at in various ways, deciphering was not necessarily a simple matter for those not in the know. John's readers were no doubt in the know, but the clue to the cryptogram, which would enable us to make an absolutely certain identification, has been lost; and so it is not surprising that none of the modern attempts to solve the cryptogram is wholly convincing. But this much seems to be certain: The number 666 is symbolic as well as cryptic. Six is a number of inferiority, whether we contrast it with seven (the number of completeness) or with eight (the sum of the numerical equivalent of the Greek letters of Jesus' name is 888). The Antichrist at his most powerful is less powerful than the incarnate Christ, Jesus; the anti-Spirit is not the equal of the Spirit of Jesus, however freely God may allow him to range (cf. 13:14-15). There can be no doubt as to where the final victory will lie, and the call for wisdom is substantially the same as the "call for the endurance and faith of the saints." (10)

The Lamb with the 144,000 on Mount Zion
14:1-5

1 Despite the fascinating force of the first beast, the Antichrist (13:1-10), and despite the deceptive persuasion of the second beast, the anti-Spirit (13:11-18), the saints have not endured and believed in vain (cf. 13:10). Despite all the machinations of satanic revolt, Christ has triumphed; God has set His King on Zion, His holy hill (Ps. 2:6). There, on the site of the palace of God's anointed King and of the temple which signifies the forgiving and saving presence of God, the place whence Israel hoped deliverance would come (Is. 59:20-21; Joel 2:32; Rom. 11:26-27)—there the prophet beholds the Lamb that was slain as Victor. With the Lamb are His own, those whom He loves and for whom He died, the whole number of God's people (144,000, cf. 7:1-8) drawn up in military order, intact and victorious. These have found that the name of the Lamb and the name of His Father are more potent than the mark and number of the beast before whom the whole world now trembles in fearful adoration.

2 They are the living and eternal refutation of the old saw which avers that the devil has all the good tunes. There bursts from them a song so bravely thunderous and in its vitality so like the unwearied figured bass of the sea that all the devil's lean and flashy songs sound, in comparison, like the squeaking and gibbering of the dead. They sing their jubilant song to the music of the harp, young David's benign dispeller of evil spirits (1 Sam. 16:14-23). 3 Their song is the newest of the new songs wherewith God's people praised Him for each new manifestation of His might and mercy (e. g., Ps. 33:3; 40:3; 96:1; 98:1; 144:9; 149:1; Is. 42:10). It is a song in praise of the King ("throne," cf. comments on 4:2) for the coming of whose kingdom His people have waited and prayed (Matt. 6:10), a song in which His creation ("living creatures," cf. comments on 4:6) and His people ("elders," cf. comments on 4:4) delight. Only the 144,000 can know and sing that song, for they have been redeemed "from the earth"; they have emerged triumphant from that haunt of sin and Satan, from the miasma which clogs and chokes man's singing in praise of his God.

4 As the men of Israel, when engaged in holy war kept themselves ceremonially pure by sexual abstinence (Deut. 23:9-10), so these soldiers of the cross have followed their Lord into battle with the untainted devotion of a virgin bride (cf. 2 Cor. 11:2-3). Their Lord's summons of "Follow me!" (Matt. 4:19; cf. John 12:26) has rung so clearly and continuously in their ear that they have not been seduced by

99

the witchery of the harlot Babylon and her "impure passion" (8; cf. 17:1-2, 5). They follow Him wherever He goes, even into death. In them the redeeming purpose of God and the Lamb has been realized (cf. 5:9); they are God's new creation, the firstfruits of His full harvest of His creation (cf. James 1:18), the beginning and the pledge of the accomplishment of the redeeming and creative purpose of Him who shall finally say, "Behold, I make all things new." (21:5)

5 Jesus promised to "the pure in heart," to men of unalloyed devotion such as these, that they should "see God" (Matt. 5:8). The presence of these men on Mount Zion with the Lamb, singing their new song before God's throne, testifies to the sure truth of the promise made to followers of the Servant who would not compromise with the lie (cf. Is. 53:9). They stand on Mount Zion with the Lamb because they have not called God's truth a lie or Satan's lie the truth and have not consented to receive the mark which brands them as servants of the father of the lie.

Three Angelic Voices and the Beatitude
on Those Who Die in the Lord
14:6-13

6 The number of those who stand on Mount Zion with the Lamb is symbolic (cf. 7:1-8), not arithmetic. The 144,000 is no closed and final figure. The number of God's saints is not yet full; therefore "the gospel must first be preached to all nations" (Mark 13:10). And preached it is, in powerful and incisive fashion. An angel "flying in midheaven," visible and audible to all the world, proclaims "to those who dwell on earth" (cf. 11:10; 13:8, 12, 14) a message which is called "an eternal gospel."

7 How can the annunciation of "the hour of God's judgment" be called good news? First, the very fact that God still speaks to a world intoxicated with the wine of Satan's lies, the fact that He does not visit men with the dread judgment of divine silence, the "famine . . . of hearing the words of the Lord" with which Amos once threatened Israel (Amos 8:11-14), that He does not yet abandon men who have abandoned Him (cf. Rom. 1:24, 26, 28), that fact is in itself a thing of grace and Gospel. Second, that He should still speak

100

to such men in the wooing and winning tones of His call to repentance, that is good news indeed. It is God's call to repentance when the angel bids men "fear God." He is inviting them to stand before God as Abraham once stood when he was ready to sacrifice his promised future at the bidding of God, to lay his future wholly into the hand of God and, trusting Him, to believe "in hope . . . against hope" (cf. Rom. 4:18; Gen. 22, esp. 22:12). He is bidding them give God glory by confessing their guilt (cf. 11:13; John 9:24; Joshua 7:19-20) and bowing before Him who is the Judge of all as surely as He is the Creator of all and holds the whole world in His hand. That an angelic voice should sound once more, in the world's last hour, the message of God's servants the prophets, the cry of John the Baptist, and Jesus' own call to His people (Matt. 3:2; 4:17; cf. Mark 6:12), the voice of God unchangingly true to Himself (cf. Hosea 11:9; Mal. 3:6)—that is eternal Gospel.

8 The proclamation of the first angel is Gospel, the power of God for man's salvation, for the rescue of man from man's desperate predicament. How desperate the predicament is, how hopeless every way but the way of repentance is, that is the burden of the second angel's proclamation. In the "eternal gospel" (6) the Word of God is being uttered, a word that will endure and stand when all competing powers wither and fall like the flowers of the field (Is. 40:6-8). Even the imposing structure reared by the anti-Trinity, even Babylon the antichurch is doomed. Its doom is so certain that the angelic voice can speak of it as already accomplished: "Fallen, fallen is Babylon." "Babylon," name of the ancient world power which put an end to the city, the anointed king, and the temple of God, has become the allusive designation for the then-current world power, Rome (cf. 1 Peter 5:13). Like Babylon, Rome the great dominates the world and persecutes and would impose her will upon the saints of God; like Babylon she corrupts what she dominates by giving men to drink of the wine of her unfaithful harlot's passion (cf. Chs. 17—19). The world city is the manufactory of all that inflames and satisfies those passions which make men unfaithful to their Creator (cf. 7) and Lord; the Creator's good gifts are put to unhallowed uses.

9 The proclamation of the third angel reinforces that of the second angel. If Babylon is doomed, there is no hope for anyone who worships the beast whose power is embodied in Babylon (cf. 17:3), for anyone who bows before the beast's image (cf. 13:14-15) and expresses his fealty to the beast by receiving his mark on forehead or hand (cf. 13:16-17). **10** On all such the third angel pronounces a terrible curse, the cast shadow of the blessing of the eternal Gospel. Two Old Testament images for the judgmental wrath of God shape the language of his curse: cup (e. g., Ps. 75:8; Is. 51:17; Jer. 25:15-16) and fire (e. g., Amos 1:4, 7, 10, 12, 14; 2:2, 5; Jer. 43:12; Hos. 8:14; Joel 2:30; Mal. 4:1). They who forget their Creator and worship the beast shall drink the untempered wine of God's wrath and shall feel the fire-and-brimstone judgment which destroyed Sodom and Gomorrah (Gen. 19:24). Their punishment is just; the angels who protect the servants of God (7:1-3), waft the prayers of all the saints into the presence of God (8:3), and to the very last have proclaimed "an eternal gospel" (6) will not intercede for them. Nor will the Lamb who loved them and died for them (1:5); He who once interceded for His excutioners (Luke 23:34) will not intercede for them. **11** Their punishment is therefore eternal. The smoke of the fire that tortures them will be an eternal monument to their unceasing torment, that grim counterpart to the unceasing tuneful adoration of "the four living creatures" at the throne of God. (4:8)

12 The time of escape and deliverance is now; the promise for those who believe and endure (cf. 13:10; Matt. 10:22) is being spoken and is to be accepted now: "*Here* is a call for the endurance of the saints." Now, in the midst of their suffering in the unequal battle with the Antichrist, the saints are called upon to keep the commandments of God (to love Him with all their heart and all their soul and all their mind, Matt. 22:37, in Jesus' words) and to follow in the footsteps of the unswerving faith of Jesus, who is "the pioneer and perfecter of our faith." (Heb. 12:2)

13 A voice from heaven repeats for them the encouraging and empowering promise. The second beatitude of Revelation (cf. 1:3) is pronounced on those who are facing death. "Henceforth," now when the struggle has grown severe and it has become clear indeed to the followers of the Lamb (cf. 4) that "we suffer with him in order that we may also be glorified with him" (Rom. 8:17). No soft pathos like that of the weeping daughters of Jerusalem (Luke 23:27-28) need bewail their end; call them blessed, says the voice from heaven, for they escape the fearful curse. Yes, call them blessed, cries the Spirit (whose word the churches must hear if they would live, cf. 2:7, 11, 17, 29; 3:6, 13, 22), for their deeds, the unforgotten record of their faith, follow them out of the toilsome infamy of this world, where beast and Babylon may reign and triumph for a while, into the bright world of rest where they shall hear their Lord's "Well done!" (Matt. 25:21, 23) and their Lord's welcoming "Come, O blessed of my Father, inherit the kingdom prepared for you." (Matt. 25:34)

The Harvest and Vintage of the Earth
14:14-20

14 These scenes (Chs. 12—14) of wild rebellion and of faithful endurance, of apparent satanic triumph and of the apparent defeat but real victory of God's servants, are not chance happenings of history. God's grace and judgment are in control, His kingdom comes, His purposes are ripening fast. The Son of Man comes with the clouds of heaven as Daniel had seen Him come (Dan. 7:13; cf. Rev. 1:7). He is already crowned for victory; no Antichrist can take from Him the glory that is His as Savior and Judge. He comes "with great power and glory" to "gather his elect" (Mark 13:26-27).

The Harvester of men has His sickle in His hand, **15-16** and at the cry of an angel who comes out of the temple (the place of God's gracious presence among His people) He swings His sickle on the earth and the full harvest of God's saints, promised and pledged by the "first fruits" already gathered in (5), is accomplished—"the earth was reaped," at God's hour and by His command. (For the harvest as an image for the ingathering of God's people, cf. Matt. 9:37-38; 13:30; Mark 4:29; Luke 10:2; John 4:35-38.)

17 Both crops, that of Christ and that of Antichrist, grow up together until the time of harvest (Matt. 13:30). The ingathering of the elect is the Son of Man's proper work (cf.

Matt. 24:30-31) and is done by His own hand. **18** The fearful, bloody harvest of the followers of Antichrist (here pictured as the vintage, in keeping with the idea of blood) is left to the angel who is in charge of God's judgmental fire. (Cf. 10)

19 He casts the ripened grapes of revolt into the great winepress of God's wrath, **20** and they are trodden out (Is. 63:3) there, outside the city of God where those inscribed in God's book shall forever dwell. Huge streams of blood well forth—the measure of that stream is a measure of the accumulated wrath of God upon hard and impenitent hearts (Rom. 2:5) and a measure, too, of the monstrosity of the guilt of those who have joined in the worldwide rebellion led by the beast.

The Fifth Vision: The Seven Bowls of Wrath
15:1—16:21

Preparation for the Pouring Out of the Seven Bowls
15:1-8

1 The "eternal gospel" of God's last call to repentance and therewith His final proffer of salvation has been announced by an angel flying in midheaven (14:6-7). But it is not only being *announced* in word to mankind from that bright sphere where the end is already being anticipated and celebrated (14:1-5). This eternal Gospel, this call to repentance, is not only being announced; it is being *enacted,* announced in deed, written into the history of mankind, unmistakably and urgently by means of a portent (cf. 12:1, 3) marked as of supreme significance by the adjectives used to describe it at its introduction ("great and wonderful"), by its designation as "the last," the plagues with which "the wrath of God is ended" (or "completed"), and by the detailed solemnity of the preparation made for its enactment. The message of the seven seals and of the seven trumpets (Chs. 4—11) is being repeated and not only repeated but intensified by the pouring-out of these climactic bowls of wrath. Will men hear and heed this last message?

The angels with the seven plagues are sent out as ministrants of God's judgment. ("Wrath" in Biblical usage does not express the freakish fury of an angered deity but is a designation of the impassioned but deliberate majesty of

104

God the Judge; cf., e. g., Rom. 2:5). **2** God's aim in sending out these ministrants of judgment is described in 2-4. He aims at the deliverance of His people. Again, as in previous visitations, the story of the exodus from Egypt supplies the materials and colors of the vision of that goal. The prophet sees not merely a repetition of the Red Sea of the first exodus but a strange "sea of glass mingled with fire." "Sea of glass" recalls the "sea of glass" (4:6) before the throne of God the Creator and Lord of all and suggests the pellucid sanctity of this last atmosphere of salvation; "fire" suggests the judicial majesty of God the Deliverer (cf. 8:5) and the "fiery ordeal" (1 Peter 4:12) through which His people must pass before they reach that shore where harp and song shall be their whole glad employ.

3 "They sing the song of Moses, the servant of God," who bade his people look to God alone for their salvation (Ex. 14:13-14). The song of Moses (Ex. 15:1) may serve as a model for the song which celebrates this final exodus, but no more than that. This song is "the song of the Lamb," the song of Him who like Moses was a witness to the God of salvation but a witness of a kind and in a degree that Moses could not be; the Lamb is a witness not only by word but in person; He is "the firstborn of the dead" (1:5), the very incarnation of that "grace and truth" which is man's salvation (John 1:17). With harps given them by God (2) the conquerors come from a victory over the beast which looked like defeat (cf. 13:7), the victory by dying which is the Lamb's own victory, and they sing the song of Moses and the Lamb, of the first deliverer and the last Deliverer (as the rabbis called Moses and the Messiah). This is the goal of all God's ways, that His people be delivered, "to the praise of his glorious grace" (Eph. 1:6). Therefore His people standing victorious at the sea of glass and fire praise Him now, in language richly reminiscent of the Old Testament (cf. Ps. 111:2, 4; 139:14; Ex. 15:11; 34:10; Deut. 32:4). They praise Him for His great and wonderful works, which only He the Almighty Lord can do—who but He could lead His people victorious from the dread onset of the beast and of the accuser (12:10) who sent and authorized the beast (13:4)? Who but He could by the cross become King of the nations?

The reading "nations," cf. footnote *j* in the RSV, is to be preferred to that in the text, "ages"; it has good ancient attestation and is more in keeping with the reminiscence of Jer. 10:6-7; 16:19-21 in v. 4:

> There is none like thee, O Lord;
>> thou art great, and thy name is great in might.
> Who would not fear thee, O King of *nations*?
>> For this is thy due;
> for among all the wise ones of the *nations*
>> and in all their kingdoms
>> there is none like thee (Jer. 10:6-7).

> O Lord . . .
> to thee shall the *nations* come
>> from the ends of the earth . . . (Jer. 16:19).

To the Crucified He has given the authority in which He sent His apostles to "all nations" (Matt. 28:19). To all nations He is manifested as the God whose ways are "just and true"— "just" in visiting man's sins upon the Crucified, "true" in being an authentic revelation of the holy God that He is, who will not execute His fierce anger against man because He is "God and not man, the Holy One." (Hos. 11:9)

4 His love, manifested in the cross, draws to Him the worship and praise of all nations, who are led to see, even in the visitation of the bowls, a part of that divine "judgment" which spoke a whole Yea of love to man in the cross, while uttering an unabridged No to all the sin of man. His redeemed people, made up of men from all nations (5:9), can but utter their praise of the judgments which reveal His glory and subserve His grace.

5 That fact that the angelic ministrants of judgment subserve God's gracious purpose of redemption is further stressed by the fact that the tent of witness and its successor, the temple, are opened. For tent and temple are the embodiment of God's promise that He would be graciously with His people: "There I will meet with the people of Israel . . . And I will dwell among the people of Israel, and will be their God. And they shall know that I am the Lord their God, who brought them forth out of the land of Egypt that I might dwell among them; I am the Lord their God" (Ex. 29:43, 45-

46). When Solomon had completed the temple, he had brought thither "the ark of the Lord, the tent of meeting, and all the holy vessels" (1 Kings 8:4), and at the dedication of the temple he prayed: "O Lord my God, hearken to the cry and to the prayer which thy servant prays before thee this day; that thy eyes may be open night and day toward this house, the place of which thou hast said, 'My name shall be there.' " (1 Kings 8:28-29)

6 From this place, expressive of God's will to be with His people, the seven angels with the seven plagues proceed. They serve to bring man into communion with his God again, by calling to repentance all who will hear and by destroying all who will not. They have a priestly office to perform and therefore wear a priestly dress, bright linen girt with gold. (Cf. Ex. 28:4, 39)

7 All creation serves God's judgmental actions (cf. 6:1, 3, 5, 7). One of the "living creatures" (cf. comments on 4:6) gives the seven angels the bowls filled with the wrath of God, who is marked as the God who in this doomed and dying world "lives for ever and ever" and will assert His holiness with undying might. **8** Before this might, half hidden by smoke (Is. 6:4) and half revealed, none can endure to stand until His mighty work be done.

The Pouring Out of the Seven Bowls of Wrath
16:1-21

1 As surely as God is the living God, His judgment will be executed completely (*"seven* bowls"). A voice from the heavenly temple (again the action is marked as subserving the redemptive purpose of God, cf. comments on 15:5) bids the seven angels be about their judgmental task on earth, to conclude the work of God's left hand—His left hand sweeps away all opposition; His right hand sets His people free.

2 The result of emptying the first bowl is described in language which recalls the sixth of the Egyptian plagues (Ex. 9:8-12). In distinction from the visitations described in the previous visions of seals and trumpets, this climactic visitation is universal in its effect; no longer is only "a fourth" (6:8) or "a third" (8:7; 9:15) of the earth or mankind affected. Climactically too, men themselves are struck at

107

once, not merely the world they inhabit. Men who have committed themselves to the beast by accepting his mark on themselves and by worshiping his image (13:15-16) are smitten by what they have loved and accepted; the mark which signifies their devotion to the beast becomes a cancerous sore to plague them. **3-4** The second bowl is poured into the sea, and the third bowl into the living waters of "the rivers and the fountains"; as at the first Egyptian plague (Ex. 7:14-24), the waters turn to blood—the addition of "of a dead man" to "blood" (3) gives this plague a touch of horror beyond that of the plague described in Ex. 7—and the sea becomes a grave to the creatures living in it.

5 Land and sea, earth and all waters, as it were, cry out in the name of the Lord of land and sea: "All things betray thee who betrayest Me."

The angel of water consents to this punitive use of the domain assigned to him, asserting the righteousness of the requital which the "Holy One," Lord of all history ("who art and wast"), in His evenhanded justice has exacted **6** from those who "have shed the blood of saints and prophets," the blood of men who have revered and proclaimed the sanctity of the life given by the Creator. They would have blood; God's justice commends the ingredients of their poisoned chalice to their own lips. He gives the bloodthirsty their due; they shall have blood to drink.

7 The animate altar, from whose base the souls of martyrs had cried for vindication (6:9-11), to which the prayers of the saints, angelically assisted, had arisen like incense to plead before God's throne (8:3-5), that altar echoes the song of Moses and the Lamb (15:3-4) in affirming God's true and righteous judgment on a world turned bestially against Him, despising the truth and righteousness which would redeem the world by His sacrifice.

8 The havoc worked by the fourth angel with the fourth bowl goes beyond any judgmental visitation recorded in the visions of the seven seals and the seven trumpets: The lot of men who have refused the seal of the living God and have accepted the mark of the beast is the opposite of the lot of God's servants. Of those protected by the seal of God it is said, "The sun shall not strike them, nor any scorching heat"

(7:16); for those wearing the mark of the beast the beneficent warmth of the sun is turned into scorching heat, before which men are defenseless. Here they must cry out, "This is the finger of God" (Ex. 8:19), and turn to face their Judge.

9 But their hard hearts will not be softened (cf. Rom. 2:5) even by this fierce heat, so obviously the work of God Himself. They curse, instead, the God who has manifested His power in these plagues ("name" implies revelation); they will not see in these visitations the beckoning hand of God that points them to repentance. They will not, even now, give God the glory due Him by confessing their guilt (cf. comments on 11:13). As the plagues symbolized by the outpouring of the bowls are climactic, so also the reaction of man is climactic. Men are no longer merely desperate (6:15-17) or simply impenitent (9:20-21); they now do what hitherto only the beast himself has done (13:5-6); they blaspheme ("curse") the God of heaven whose call to repentance they reject.

10 The fifth bowl, like the first (2) strikes the antichristian power; not, however, in the persons of the committed worshipers of the beast but in the visible and palpable institutional symbol of the power of the beast, the "throne" where he is seated and reigns. A darkness like that of the ninth Egyptian plague, a darkness so oppressive as "to be felt" (Ex. 10:21), enwraps the kingdom of the beast. Only "the sun of righteousness" (Mal. 4:2), rising on those who fear God's name, can dispel that darkness; but even in their dark anguish, which makes them gnaw their tongues, men will not fear Him who has stricken them. **11** They will not seek the healing in His wings (Mal. 4:2); instead, they curse Him, "the God of heaven" (Dan. 2:19), for the "pain and sores" He has inflicted on them for their good, and will not turn in repentance from their darkling deeds.

12 The outpouring of the sixth bowl is described in more detail than any heretofore; it does not introduce an immediate visitation but only the *preparation* for the great final war against God, described in 19:19-21. The preparation is ominous enough. The sixth bowl is emptied upon the river Euphrates. The Euphrates marked the eastern limit of Israel's land (Gen. 15:18; Deut. 1:7)—could aught of blessing

109

lie beyond that line? John's readers might recall that Isaiah had threatened his people with overwhelming judgment from that river (Is. 8:5-8). And men of the Roman Empire looked fearfully toward that eastern region whose mounted hordes perpetually threatened the security of the Roman peace. At the outpouring of the sixth bowl the watery barrier of the Euphrates is removed; now the way is clear for the invasion of the kings from the East.

13 Whatever the historical identity of these kings may be, one thing is clear: They are inspired to this motion by the foul, clammy spirits that proceed from the anti-Trinity, the desperate enemies of God. Why they are likened to frogs is not easily made out; one whose mind is so filled with the Old Testament (and especially with the story of the exodus) as the prophet John's could hardly fail to think of the Egyptian plague of frogs (Ex. 8:1-15). Elsewhere in the religious world round about the New Testament, too, frogs were regarded as ill-omened creatures. Perhaps it is enough to see in these unclean (cf. Lev. 11:9-12), cold creatures the extreme opposite of the pure brightness and warmth of the "seven spirits of God" portrayed as flaming torches casting their glow before the throne of God (4:5). Certainly the inspiring power of the anti-Spirit is thought of here; the second beast is here for the first time called "false prophet"; he lives and acts in the false words which he inspires men to speak. **14** These spirits, demonic in their imitation of and opposition to the divine, act as couriers of the anti-Trinity, to summon all royal powers in the world to unite in battle against "God the Almighty" on "the great day" when He shall rise up in His omnipotence to bring low "all that is proud and lofty . . . all that is lifted up and high." (Is. 2:12; cf. Is. 2:13-22)

15 The mention of "the great day of God" (familiar to the church from the Old Testament) would seem to promise that the end and victory are near; but the church has no reason to relax her vigilance on that account. The huge and fearful forces now being mustered cannot shake the Almighty from His throne, but they can work mischief on a church grown lax and negligent. Therefore the voice of Christ is heard, quite unexpectedly, renewing His warning to His own that they be vigilant (Matt. 24:43). The great day of God will come "suddenly" (Mark 13:36; Luke 21:34). The time and season of the final victory remain unknown and incalculable (Matt. 24:36). The only posture for the church is therefore the posture of glad and ready vigilance; the alternative is exposure and shame—on the day which God intends to be the day of "the revealing of the sons of God." (Rom. 8:19; cf. 1 John 3:2; Matt. 13:43)

16 The evil spirits of the anti-Trinity gather the levied kings of the earth to a place called, mysteriously and suggestively, Armageddon; it is so called "in Hebrew," which suggests an Old Testament connection. Just what the Old Testament connection is remains unclear. Some scholars have thought of the "hill of assembly" and find in "Armageddon" an allusion to Is. 14:13-14. In that passage, a taunt-song against the king of Babylon, the proud and impious king is represented as expressing his rebellious pride in the words

> I will ascend to heaven;
> above the stars of God
> I will set my throne on high;
> I will sit on the *mount of assembly* . . .
> I will make myself like the Most High.

This would fit in well with the proud defiance of God which finds expression in the projected campaign of the kings of the whole world, but it does not explain sufficiently the Greek form of the word (Armageddon).

Others render the word as a transliteration of two Hebrew words meaning "his fruitful mountain" or "the desirable city," referring to Mount Zion or to Jerusalem respectively. There is a certain plausibility in either suggestion: It is on Mount Zion that the Lamb has appeared (14:1) with His troops prepared for holy war (cf. comments on 14:4), and in 20:9 the last attack of Satan's forces is directed against "the beloved city," Jerusalem.

Still others refer "Armageddon" to Mount Carmel, translating "the mountain of Megiddo." The town Megiddo lay some 6 miles from the southern end of Mount Carmel. At Megiddo Barak and Deborah had overthrown the vastly superior forces led by Sisera, general of the Canaanite king Jabin (Judg. 5:19). An allusion to that signal and unexpected victory, in which the seemingly doomed forces of the Lord triumphed over impossible odds, would be fitting here in Revelation 16, where the vast levy of the kings inspired by the Antichrist seems to make improbable a victory by the people of the Lord. But, on the other hand, Mount Carmel is nowhere else call "the mountain of Megiddo" as one might expect since The Revelation to John itself offers no explanation of the name. Besides, it is intrinsically unlikely that Mount Carmel should be identified by means of a reference to a town so far from the mountain itself, lying in ruins since 350 B. C. and fallen into oblivion by the time when The Revelation to John was written. All of these (and other) interpretations remain uncertain; it may be that John and his readers possessed a clue to the significance and connotation of the name, but that clue seems to have been lost to us, though the term "Armageddon" as a designation for "any great climactic conflict" has passed into common English usage.

17 The seventh bowl is emptied. The seventh bowl does not, like the seventh seal and the seventh trumpet, serve merely as a transition to succeeding visions (cf. 8:1, 6; 11:15). The promise given by the angel "that there should be no more delay" (10:6) is being fulfilled; and the cry which rings from the temple and the throne of God, "It is done!" signifies that the promise of 15:1 ("the wrath of God is ended") is also being fulfilled. The wrath of God strikes the lower air, where the unholy spirit which inspires disobedience has his haunt. (Eph. 2:2)

18 The terrifying phenomena which marked the appearance of God at Sinai and made His people tremble (Ex. 19:16) are seen and heard once more, augmented by an earthquake of unprecedented violence. **19** The aggregates and habitations of men are stricken. "The great city" (probably "the great city" of 11:8, the holy city no longer holy since its people crucified the Lord) is cleft in three. The cities of the nations, whence the kings of the whole world have been summoned for their concerted attack on God—they fall too. And "Babylon the great" (14:8)—her greatness is doomed. God, the remembering Witness against the antichurch, has not forgotten great Babylon; the fury of His wrath will find her out. (The theme of Chs. 17—19 is here being announced.)

20 The islands and mountains, the fixed geographical points by which sailors set their courses, disappear. One cannot find one's way in this shaken world. **21** Huge hailstones from heaven strike mankind. "I smote you . . . yet you did not return to me," the Lord once complained through Amos (Amos 4:9). Nor do men turn now to the God who has smitten them; once more (cf. 16:9, 11) we hear how men consummate their satanic revolt by cursing God.

The Sixth Vision: The Fall of Babylon
and the Victory over Antichrist
17:1—19:21

With the emptying of the seventh bowl (16:17) "the wrath of God is ended" (15:1), that is, the surface operation of God's judicial reaction to the revolt of man and man's blasphemous hostility to Him has reached its close and conclusion. Yet, the revolt of man is but the surface eruption of the deeper subsurface hostility of the powers operative in history, the satanic powers of the anti-Trinity (the dragon, Ch. 12; the first and the second beast, Ch. 13; and the still-to-be-depicted power of the antichurch, Babylon, Ch. 17). Not that these are two separate histories, the human and the satanic; we have rather, in these visions, two views of one history, the surface and the subsurface view. And there have been indications that the surface view rests on the revelation of the presence and power of uncanny subsurface hostilities: The two witnesses of God are assailed and apparently overcome by "the beast that ascends from the bottomless pit" (11:7), the Antichrist; the bowls of wrath are emptied not only upon man's world and man but also upon the throne and kingdom of the beast (16:10); "foul spirits like frogs" (16:13) proceeding from the anti-Trinity are the demonic animus of the kings of the world gathered for battle against God at Armageddon (16:14, 16); Babylon, counterpart and opponent of the church, has already been twice marked out for destruction (14:8;

16:19). The reaction of God's wrath upon these profounder powers, hinted at previously, is to be depicted in 17:1—20:10.

The hostile powers appear in the order: dragon (Ch. 12), the two beasts (Ch. 13), and Babylon (Ch. 17). They go down before the annihilating wrath of God in the reverse order: first Babylon (Chs. 17—18), then the two beasts (19:20), and then the dragon, or Satan (20:10). "Babylon" is the point at which the surface and the subsurface realities meet; for John and his readers that point presented itself in the oppressive splendor and power of Rome. The visitation of God's wrath on Babylon is therefore treated first and at length (Chs. 17—18). If the Eternal City (as Rome was called) be revealed as subject to the wrath of the eternal God, what room is there, in a world made clean by God's judgment, for the beasts? Their fate is therefore told almost casually, with impressive brevity (19:20). The fate of Satan himself is more fully told, as a part of the ultimate triumph of God (20:1-10) in connection with the Last Judgment and God's gorgeous renewal of His world.

The Mystery of the Woman and the Beast
17:1-6a

1 The vision of the seven bowls has concluded with a reference to the judgment on Babylon (16:19), and it is an angel from among the number of those who poured out the seven bowls who introduces the vision of the judgment (that is, both the condemnation and the punishment) of Babylon, the great harlot. The antichurch is pictured as a woman, to mark both the parallel with and the contrast to the church. While the church, the people of God, has been pictured as the mother of the Messiah (Ch. 12) and will again appear as a woman, as the bride of Christ (19:7-8; 21:2, 9), the antichurch is pictured as a harlot, as a woman bound by no ties and committed to no loyalties. Harlotry and fornication (2) were familiar Old Testament figures of immorality and infidelity to the Lord, the God of Israel (cf., e. g., Is. 1:21; Jer. 2:20; Ezek. 16:15-52; Hos. 2:2-13). One recalls that the prophetess of Thyatira was called Jezebel (2:20), to brand her satanic profundities (2:24) as "harlotries" (2 Kings 9:22).

114

Like ancient Babylon, she is described, with a phrase of Jeremiah's, as dwelling "by many waters" (Jer. 51:13), in Jeremiah an allusion to the Babylonian system of irrigation canals, here interpreted to mean "peoples and multitudes and nations and tongues" (15) in allusion to Rome's far-flung mercantile empire which made her "rich in treasures" (Jer. 51:13; cf. Rev. 18:11-19). This harlot is a figure of worldwide significance and influence. **2** Kings of the earth have purchased her favors by submitting to her power and by accepting her vices and idolatries. (It becomes increasingly clear that in portraying the harlot Babylon the prophet has his eye on Rome, the city of seven hills, cf. 9. The whole empire aped Rome and got drunk on her vicious wine.)

3 "In the Spirit," caught up by the Spirit's power and illumined by His wisdom, the prophet is carried by the angel "into a wilderness" (Isaiah had prophetically witnessed the fall of ancient Babylon from the vantage point of the wilderness, Is. 21:1-9), and he sees the harlot at close range. She is seated, as ancient goddesses were sometimes portrayed as seated, on a beast whose color, scarlet, suggests the eye-catching magnificence of the Roman Empire; the beast's "blasphemous names," as well as his "seven heads and ten horns," serve to identify him with the beast rising from the sea (13:1), the Antichrist. Antichrist and antichurch belong together; the antichurch is supported by the power and organization of the Antichrist.

4 The harlot is dressed in imperial purple and in screaming scarlet (in contrast perhaps to the pure whiteness of Christ and His "armies of heaven," 19:11-14). She is bedizened with gold, precious stones, and pearls; her costly garniture is from the earth and sea, from below in contrast to the heavenly splendor with which the woman who bore the Messiah is decked out (12:1). Is it far-fetched to see in the golden cup which she extends, a "cup full of abominations and the impurities of her fornication," the abominable counterpart to "the cup of blessing" (1 Cor. 10:16) which the church extends to her own?

5 On her forehead she, like a Roman prostitute, wears a headband on which her name is inscribed. Her name is "a name of mystery," a name which only one enlightened by the Spirit can know and understand. Who could divine, unaided, that the power which Paul could proclaim as being "from God" (Rom. 13:1) and as serving His beneficent purpose in the world, is, or can become, the harlot proffering her seductive cup and tempting others into a harlotry like her own ("mother of harlots")?

6a When her seduction fails, when remembering men drink the cup of blessing and remain singly loyal to the Lord who died for them, the harlot's seduction turns into ferocity; the prophet sees her "drunk with the blood of saints," of men so wholly claimed and consecrated by God that they remain unmoved by the harlot's solicitations. She revels in the death of men who witness to their Lord and die in witnessing, "the martyrs of Jesus." In speaking of the harlot as *drunk* with the blood of saints, the prophet may be recalling the intoxicated fury of a Nero, who had A. D. 64 made a carnival of his killing of Christians, wrapping them in the skins of wild animals, that they might be torn by hunting dogs, or making living torches of their crucified bodies to illuminate his gardens.

Interpretation of the Mystery of the Woman and the Beast 17:6b-18

6b The prophet marveled at what he saw; and well he might. He had been promised a vision of "the judgment of the great harlot" (1). What he saw, this figure of power and voluptuous vitality, capable of turning in intoxicated fury upon any who refused her seductive cup or opposed her will, did not look like one on whom judgment has been pronounced and executed; far from it. **7** Therefore the angel proceeds to interpret the mystery of the woman mounted on the seven-headed, ten-horned beast. The fact that he dwells on the significance of the beast is another indication of how organically close the connection between beast and harlot, Antichrist and antichurch, is. They can be known and understood only together.

8 The interpretation of the figure of the beast is cryptic, a sort of cryptogram to which John's first readers probably possessed the key. The key is for us only partially recoverable. It seems clear that Rome, the succession of Roman emperors, and ten kings who have become vassals of the Roman Empire constitute the historical background and furnish the colors for the prophetic interpretation of God's ways in history. The beast who is to ascend from the bottomless pit is the Antichrist known from Chs. 12 and 13 (cf. 11:7); he is both Antichrist and pseudo-Christ, for in his history he is an uncanny imitation of Him who can say of Himself, "I died, and behold I am alive for evermore" (1:18). The beast too "was and is not and is to come"; he will have a "coming" which is deceptively similar to the "coming" of Christ (cf. 2 Thess. 2:8-9). But he is a doomed pseudo-Christ; he does not possess "the keys of Death and Hades," the authority to release men from death and Hades, as Christ has (1:18)—though there is in his lie a potent infusion of the truth of Christ, the Conqueror of death, enough to have power to draw to himself in marveling wonder the dwellers on earth who think earthly things (for the connotation of "dwellers on earth," cf. 11:10; 13:8, 12, 14; 17:2). Only God's eternally elective love can preserve men from this fatal fascination; only those whose names are written in His book of life can escape the fascination of the beast.

9 To such the Spirit of God will give wisdom. They are enabled, through the prophet's word, to recognize in the seven heads of the beast the seven hills of Rome on which the antichurch currently has her seat. **10** And, since Rome is not only a geographic entity but also a political one, they can also recognize in the seven heads persons in power. "Kings" was a common designation for Roman emperors (cf. 1 Peter 2:17, where the RSV rightly translates the Greek word for "king" with "emperor"), and it is natural to think of them here. But all attempts to fit the known Roman emperors up to the time of Domitian (or Nero) into the scheme of v. 10 are beset by difficulties and uncertainties; it would therefore seem the wiser course (as being in keeping with the use of numbers in Revelation generally) to look upon the numbers as symbolic rather than arithmetic. The Roman emperors (and especially Nero and Domitian) provide the current color and a recognizable contemporary point of attachment for the prophecy concerning the antichristian powers at work A. D. 95 in Asia, but the content is more then they. "Antichrist" has many incarnations (cf. 1 John 2:18). The message of the prophet John is, then, not merely a diagrammatic representation of the history and threat of the Roman Empire, however much it may be colored by the experience of the church under the Empire and may speak of the antichristian power in terms of that experience (as an American might say, "No President can set the black man free; only God can do that," clearly alluding to Abraham Lincoln but equally clearly not confining his utterance to the tragic history of the black man in America). What the prophet has to tell the martyr church is no easy optimism, no "things are bound to get better by and by." The power of the beast (currently visible in the Empire) marches through history powerfully and impressively, but is nonetheless marked by imperfection all the way. Five emperors have come and gone, fallen men whose number, *five*, falls short of the number of completeness, seven; a sixth (still short of seven), who has not yet come, is destined when he comes to abide only a little while—Satan's time is short (12:12), and the time of successful antichristian power is likewise limited.

11 The seventh is the very incarnation of the power of Antichrist, clothed in pseudo-Christian awe, and he is, apparently, a horrible contradiction to the law of the divine control of history; he is the *eight,* exceeding the number set by God even though he belongs to the number of the seven who have preceded him, an inhuman human figure. It may be that the allusion is to Domitian as an intensified Nero come again. But though he may appear to have escaped, as the eighth, the divine law that governs history by *seven's*, he is doomed. He "goes to perdition" like the rest. The great exception proves to be no exception after all. He who sits upon the throne (cf. Ch. 4) remains seated there, majestically and imperturbably in control of even this "exceptional" history. The church may take note, for her comfort: The Antichrist, that beast who sustains the persecuting antichurch, may survive and revive with amazing vitality and doughtiness, but his end is perdition nevertheless.

118

12 The beast who supports and sustains the harlot Babylon has seven heads and *ten horns* (3). The political strength and resources of the Antichrist have not, therefore, been fully enumerated in the interpretation of the seven heads as seven "kings." The Roman imperial might was reinforced and augmented by the submission of vassal kings, and the vassal kings gained in power and influence by their submission to the empire. They, too, belong to the picture which portrays the source of power and the secret of the fate of the antichurch. These vassal kings no longer have the autonomous royal power which was natively theirs; but they have found a useful substitute for it in their alliance with the beast, albeit a temporary one, one bound to fail when the "one hour" allotted by God is past.

13 Their alliance with the beast is effected by their becoming subject to the beast; with mysterious unanimity they "give over their power and authority" to it. **14** The beast's desperate purpose has become their purpose: to wage war against the Lamb, the Opposite and the Opponent of all the beast stands for (cf. 16:12-16; 19:11-21). But all their conglomerated power is not enough to stay the victory of Him who bears the title of God Himself, "Lord of lords and King of kings" (cf. Deut. 10:17; Dan. 2:47; 4:17). His love it was that chose His followers in the fight; His word has called them and inspired them for the battle; they cannot but prove faithful in the fray.

15 Though the kings summon to their aid all the "peoples and multitudes and nations and tongues" that eddy like great waters round the harlot's throne (cf. Jer. 47:2), they cannot prevail. Indeed, they are carrying out, all unwittingly, the judgmental purpose of God.

16 With a hatred as satanically irrational as their former devotion has been, they turn upon the harlot who once charmed them and made them drunk, to ravage and destroy her. **17** They cannot know that the word of God, the only valid and effective power in history (cf. Is. 40:6-8), controls them all the way, both in their unanimous submission to the beast and in their savage revenge upon the harlot. **18** The "great city," the world religion created and fostered by conquerors and subject kings in order to unite and preserve the world empire, has in it the seeds of its own destruction and is doomed.

The Annunciation of the Fall of Babylon
18:1-3

1 God has "remembered great Babylon, to make her drain the cup of the fury of his wrath" (16:19). Again (cf. 14:8) an angel's voice is heard announcing the fall of Babylon; but the angel is not now traversing midheaven as he cries. The judgment is near, and the heralding angel is the close forerunner of judgment; he comes down from heaven, and his attendant splendor makes bright the earth. Through acts of judgment, too, God is revealed; He clears the way for His Gospel by removing and annihilating the powers that oppose Him, and so His kingdom comes, His name is hallowed, and His will is done.

2 There is no mistaking the angel's message. His mighty voice proclaims, in terms that recall Isaiah's oracles of doom on ancient Babylon (Is. 13; 21:9), the fall of the great city and the resulting desolate horror of the site of this once-brilliant metropolis. Demons, foul spirits, and abominable birds, those lovers of desolate places, now haunt the scenes of thronging power and splendor, **3** and the angel's voice recounts once more the reason for the fall of the city: God can endure no longer the havoc she has created among the nations by the impure passion which her cup (17:4) inspires or by the ambition and avarice fanned into flame in kings and merchants by her harlotry.

"Come out of her, my people"
18:4-8

4-5 Another voice (probably the voice of Christ, since it speaks of God in the third person, 5, 8, yet speaks of the saints as "*my* people") bids God's people (the word used for "people" is the word regularly used in the New Testament to indicate *God's* people in contrast to "the nations," Gentiles) depart from doomed Babylon (cf. Jer. 51:45-46). They are not to share in her sins or in her deserved plagues. Deserved plagues they are. Her mounting sins have reached high heaven; and God, the living Rememberer of iniquities (cf.

16:19), will punish her for her iniquities. It is the miracle of God's long-suffering grace that there should be in this city men who can be addressed as "my people" and can be spared amid the judgment visited upon Babylon. One is reminded how the Lord once told Paul at Corinth, of all places: "There are many in this city who are my people." (Acts 18:10 NEB)

6 The voice from heaven commands that Babylon be left to the wrath of God (cf. 8). Whether the voice is addressing (unnamed) ministers of God's wrath or is bidding the people of God to "come out" from Babylon so completely that there shall not be left even ten righteous in the city to shield her from God's wrath (Gen. 18:32), one can hardly make out. But it is clear that the full rigor of the Law, eye for an eye, tooth for a tooth, is to be applied doubly to her who has flouted the Law. She shall drink double of the fatal wine which she has mixed for others (for the cup as a symbol of judgment, cf. Ps. 75:7-8). **7-8** She who glorified herself and refused to give God His glory (cf. 11:13) shall see a sorry end to her own glory; she who, like ancient Babylon (Is. 47:7-8), vaunted her queenly, immutable autonomy and exulted in her own might shall come to know the God of judgment as One mightier than herself.

The Threefold Lament over Babylon
18:9-19

9-10 The horror of the mighty city's improbable and unexpected fall is brought home to the reader by a dramatic presentation of the lament excited by her fall in kings (9-10), in princely (cf. 23) merchants (11-17a), and in all the lesser folk ("shipmasters and seafaring men, sailors and all whose trade is on the sea") who once fed, and were fed by, her insatiable love of luxury (17b-19). The language is strongly Old Testamental, recalling the dirges over Tyre uttered of old by Isaiah (Is. 23) and Ezekiel (Ezek. 27). The kings of the earth who once courted the harlot Babylon now stand afar off from her with whom they once sought intimacy and weep and wail, intimidated by her torment and the sight of the smoke which rises from the fires of her judgment (which they themselves have helped kindle, cf. 17:16-18), fires by which the words of God are fulfilled. They have seen how little the might of mighty Babylon has availed her in the quick catastrophe of God's judgment.

11 "The merchants of the earth," merchantlike, bewail the loss of trade—"no one buys their cargo any more"; and merchantlike they take inventory of their loss, lingering over the list of good things gone useless: **12-13** precious metals, costly clothing, things of delectable taste and scent, thronging livestock, "horses and chariots" that make a braggart prancing for man, and—the harshest word spoken on slavery in the New Testament marks the brutality underlying this costly show—"slaves, that is, human souls."

14 The shallowness and emptiness of a life that lives on these things is cruelly illustrated by this verse: The fruit market is gone—and the city is made desolate thereby. The city and the suppliers of her desire learn too late that "all that is in the world, the lust of the flesh and the lust of the eyes and the pride of life"—all the sleek and splendid things they have settled for—are "of the world," which "passes away" (1 John 2:16-17). **15-17a** Like the rich man in Jesus' story (Luke 16:19-31) they learn too late and to their sorrow and terror that purple and fine linen and all such gear are lost forever in that "one hour" when God reverses all.

17b All the shipmasters who once were drawn, as by a mighty magnet, toward Babylon now stand afar off **18** and cry out over the conflagration which marks the site of the once incomparable and venerated (cf. 13:4) city. **19** They throw dust on their heads in token of their grief for her who was once the source of sailors' wealth, now suddenly and summarily laid waste.

"Rejoice over Her!"
18:20

20 A voice, not identified but clearly not that of the seafaring folk of 17b-19, breaks into this noise of lamentation with a summons to rejoice over fallen Babylon, that fearful and pernicious caricature of the church. Heaven, abode of God the enthroned King (4:3), is told to rejoice; and all those whose eyes have been fixed heavenward, not turned toward alluring Babylon, are to join in heaven's rejoicing: the saints whose prayers have implored God for the coming of this His day (8:3-5); the apostles whose names are to be inscribed on the foundations of the new, heavenly Jerusalem (21:14), who even now hold citizenship in heaven (Phil 3:20); the prophets to whom a door in heaven has been opened in order that they might make strong their brethren with the message of what they there beheld (4:1; cf. 1:10, 19). They may all rejoice, not with an all-too-human gloating over a fallen enemy, but because God in His love has triumphed over Babylon's bestial self-seeking will; *He*, by the divine verdict which destroyed Babylon, has vindicated the cause of those who looked to Him.

The Millstone Thrown into the Sea:
The Desolation of Babylon
18:21-24

21 The whole of the vision of the judgment on Babylon—the annunciation of her fall (1-3), the warning to God's people (4-8), the laments over Babylon's fall (9-19), the appeal to heaven and all heavenly ones to rejoice over her fall (20)—is deeply indebted, in language and imagery, to the Old Testament. The prophet John speaks (naturally and almost inevitably, it seems) the language of the prophets who were spokesmen for God before him. The last scene of the vision, the hurling by a mighty angel of "a stone like a great millstone" into the sea as a symbol of the desolating destruction of the great city, is also derived from the Old Testament, from the book of the prophet Jeremiah. After Jeremiah had written in a book "all the evil that should come upon Babylon" (Jer. 51:60), he instructed Seraiah, the transmitter of his book, to "bind a stone to it and cast it into the midst of the Euphrates" with the words (from the Lord): "Thus shall Babylon sink, to rise no more, because of the evil that I am bringing upon her" (Jer. 51:63-64). The vision of John is an extension and enlargement of this theme from Jeremiah—not a Judaic quartermaster (Jer. 51:59) but a mighty angel takes up the symbol of judgment, the great millstone, and he hurls it down, not into the river Euphrates but into the world-engirdling sea, with words that pronounce

123

definitive judgment: Violently the violent city shall be thrown down, and her fall is for ever.

22 In times of disaster men comfort themselves with dreams of a time to come when "things will be normal again" and old dear familiarities can be resumed. The angel bids Babylon to forgo that dream; there will be for her no normal times again. The old songs will not be sung again, and the old sweet music will not be made anymore. The longed-for hum of human industry will not be made anymore; the busy sounds of craftsmen thumping and hammering are gone, and gone the steady hum of millstones grinding grain for daily bread. **23** The streets of darkened Babylon will never know again the snug hour when evening lamps are lit. The ever-new rapturous voice of bride and bridegroom will not be heard again. The time of weddings is past. The mournful words of the mighty angel sound like a dirge over the death of human culture—what lovely gifts of God are lost when men use them against the God who gave them! Music, the arts and crafts, marriage—Babylon has used her gifts to exalt men and to bewitch and deceive them. **24** And to destory those who would not be deceived: the prophets who spoke God's word faithfully, the saints who would not break God's spell upon them, all those who in their dying bore witness on earth to the Lord of the earth. Babylon cannot bend her past out of its eternal shape; that shape is guilt, blood-guilt on a worldwide scale.

Hallelujah! For the Lord Our God Almighty Reigns
19:1-10

1 The *summons* to rejoice over the fall of Babylon has been heard as early as 18:20, where the lament over fallen Babylon is followed by the imperative:

> Rejoice over her, O heaven,
> O saints and apostles and prophets,
> for God has given judgment for you against her!

The *rejoicing* itself finds expression in the threefold hallelujah (1, 3, 6) of 19:1-8. The prophet hears a great multitude, the great victorious multitude of 7:9, jubilantly expanding the sense of "Hallelujah!" (the Hebrew word means "Praise the Lord!") by attributing to the Lord God the positive results of His judgmental action—salvation, power, and glory: the salvation He has wrought, the power He has evinced, the glory He has manifested 2 by His true and just judgment upon the harlot, the corrupter of His very good creation (the earth and the dwellers therein), and by His vindication of His slaughtered servants. Their cry for vindication, stilled into patience at 6:9-11, has not been answered. 3 The ever-rising smoke of Babylon's conflagration attests the eternity of God's judgment upon her.

4 The church and all creation (represented before the throne of God by "the twenty-four elders and the four living creatures," cf. 4:4, 6) in beatific prostration confirm ("Amen!") and echo the universal praise of the multitude's "Hallelujah!"; 5 and a voice from the very throne of God (the voice of God the King) encourages all God's reverent and obedient servants to continue

the song, the heavenly song
the Lord of all things loves.

6 This voice is answered by the reverberating and shattering joyful noise of the third hallelujah uttered in praise of the Almighty who has heard the cry of those who prayed, "Thy kingdom come!" and has made their night of weeping to be followed by the morn of song. 7 They cannot but give Him His proper glory in their joyously exultant song, for He has ended the time of fasting that began when the Bridegroom was taken from them (cf. Matt. 9:15) and has given them feasting for fasting at the marriage feast of the Lamb. 8 His love provides the feast; and His love decks out the "Bride," the church, for the feast. The "fine linen, bright and pure," wherewith the church has decked herself for this ultimate communion with her Lord is His gift to her. The "righteous deeds of the saints" are the gift of Him who is at work in His saints that they may "both will and work for his good pleasure." (Phil. 2:12-13)

9 The angel who has introduced (17:1) and interpreted (17:7) the vision of the judgment of the great harlot pronounces the fourth of the seven beatitudes of The Revelation to John (cf. 1:3; 14:13; 16:15; 20:6; 22:7, 14). The

vision which portrays the judgment upon the harlot Babylon and pronounces doom on all who drink of her abominable cup closes with the bright prospect of the church's consummated union and communion with her Lord and pronounces a divine blessing ("These are true words of God") on all who have heeded the "true words of God" as His invitation to the marriage supper. (Cf. Matt. 25:1-13)

10 Overwhelmed by the majesty and mercy of the angel's message, the prophet falls at his feet and is ready to pay him divine honors, to worship him. But the angel will not permit him to honor the created messenger rather than the Creator (cf. Rom. 1:25). The angel takes his place among the servants of God, alongside the prophet and alongside those who, by hearing and keeping the words of his prophecy (1:3), hold fast the testimony of the faithful Witness (1:5), who testified in deed and word that man owes his God a whole worship in undivided love and loyalty (cf. Matt. 4:1-11; 22:34-40). His testimony inspires all prophecy and makes impossible for the prophet any worship which is not worship of God alone.

The Victory of the Word
of God over the Antichrist
19:11-21

11 In the vision of God Enthroned the prophet had beheld "in heaven an open door" (4:1); at the blast of the seventh trumpet when loud voices in heaven proclaimed, "The kingdom of the world has become the kingdom of our Lord and of his Christ" (11:15), and the 24 elders proclaimed that the time had come "for destroying the destroyers of the earth" (11:17-18), the prophet had beheld "God's temple in heaven . . . opened, and the ark of his covenant . . . within his temple" (11:19). Now, in the vision which climaxes the destruction of the destroyer Babylon together with the destruction of the two beasts who supported and inspired Babylon (19:19-20), now he beholds all heaven opened (cf. Ezek. 1:1) and sees a Rider on a white horse. This victorious Rider is the antithesis of the rider he had seen before (6:2). This is not the Antichrist, that imitator and opponent of Christ who was permitted to go forth "conquering and to conquer" a world in love with the lie (cf. 2 Thess. 2:10-11). This Rider is One whose names mark Him as One whom men may trust ("Faithful") and as One whom men may believe ("True," cf. 3:14). He is the promised "shoot from the stump of Jesse," the Messiah of whose coming Isaiah had spoken (Is. 11:1-10); He was to usher in a reign of paradisal peace (Is. 11:6-8) by a righteous judgment which vindicates and delivers the poor while it destroys the wicked (Is. 11:3-4). Even so this Rider judges and makes war "in righteousness," in compassionate fidelity to the covenant of God. **12** No wrong done by any destroyer of the earth can escape the scrutiny of His fiery eyes (cf. 1:14; 2:18); no power can resist the many-diademed royalty of this Judge and Warrior, whose name is without analogy and therefore incommunicable to man—"No one knows the Son except the Father," this Bearer of the ineffable name said in the days of His flesh. (Matt. 11:27)

13 What communion of human sonship can compare with the communion between this One and His Father, this One who is so purely a part of His Father as a man's word is a part, as it is the expression, of the man himself? "The Word of God," the One in whom God has uttered His will that men shall live, and live in the light (cf. John 1:1-5)—that is the name by which He is called. And so, inevitably, He comes to the battle as One already victorious, His robe already dipped in the blood of His conquered enemies (cf. Is. 63:1-6)—or it may be that "the blood of his servants" (19:2) who, with their own robes washed white in His blood, have shed their blood in faithful witness to Him (cf. 12:11) marks Him as the unconquerable Leader of an unconquerable army.

14 The armies of heaven, the martyr-conquerors named so often in this book of prophecy (cf., e. g., 2:7, 11, 17, 26; 3:5, 12, 21; 12:11; 15:2; 21:7), follow in His train; they are clad, not in the armor of battle but in pure white linen, the festal array of victory, and ride upon the white horses of victory. **15** They have good grounds for their confidence in the victory of their Lord. He is portrayed in Old Testament imagery that betokens might and victory, imagery of the Messianic King (Is. 11:4; Ps. 2:9) and of the Lord God Himself (Is. 63:3; Joel 3:13). He will do the work of God Almighty, treading the

127

winepress of the fury of the wrath of God against all those who dare oppose the King whom He has set upon His holy hill. **16** And so the name inscribed upon the Rider's robe, visible where the robe is spread flat against His thigh, is the divine name, "King of kings and Lord of lords" (cf. Deut. 10:17; Dan. 2:47)—no kingly power and no lordly might of man or Satan can escape His rod of iron. The deified Roman emperor may call himself (and be called by his subjects) "God and Lord," but those grandiloquent titles ring hollow at the coming of this Rider on the white horse.

17 Torrential and thunderous voices of a great multitude had sung of "the marriage of the Lamb" (19:6-7), and an angel had pronounced a beatitude on those invited to His "marriage supper" (19:9). An angel standing in the sun issues a grim counterpart to that invitation when he bids "the birds that fly in midheaven . . . gather for the great supper of God" (cf. Ezek. 39:4, 17-20), **18-19** to gorge themselves on the flesh of the enemies of God both great and small, fallen in their vain attack upon the King of kings and Lord of lords. This is what the concerted attack of the forces of Antichrist comes to; it provides a carrion feast for birds of prey. Kings, captains, mighty men, horsemen and horses with their own flesh feed the birds of prey. There is in this an echo, as it were, of the derisive laughter of Him who sits in heaven and declares to the enemies who conspire against His Anointed: "I have set my king on Zion, my holy hill" (Ps. 2:4-6). Derisive, too, is the sparseness of the narrative which recounts the defeat of that mighty host of kings and commoners who long have planned this attack (16:12-14; 17:13-14) on the Rider of the white horse.

20 One verse suffices to tell how the beast and the false prophet (who inspired the lying signs and wonders which gave the beast his mystic hold on men) were captured and thrown alive into the sulphurous fire "prepared for the devil and his angels" (Matt. 25:41). **21** The fate of their followers is no less sparsely told. The Rider with the ineffable name (12) evinces His deity in that He speaks and it is done; His word, "the sword that issues from his mouth" (cf. 1:16; Is. 49:2), slays them—and birds gorge themselves on the slain men's flesh. The Gospel proves to be "a fragrance from death to death" (2 Cor. 2:16) to all its enemies.

Antichurch, Antichrist, and anti-Spirit have fallen. There remains the anti-God, the devil, to be cleared away; then the last judgment comes, followed by God's new world.

The Seventh Vision: Judgment and Renewal
20:1—22:5

The Overthrow of Satan: The Thousand Years
20:1-10

In the vision of the beginning of the end, when the Messianic Child destined to rule all the nations was born, the attack of Satan on the Child is marked as foredoomed to failure from the first. Satan cannot, for all his star-confounding fury (12:4), devour the Child. The Child is "caught up to God and to his throne" (12:5). Satan storms heaven in vain and loses forever his place as unresting accuser of mankind (12:7-11). Thrown down to earth, he vents his fury (a fury all the more intense because he knows his time is short, 12:12), upon the woman from whom the Messiah came, the people of God. Again in vain; the woman is kept and nourished in the wilderness (12:14). And when Satan attacks the people of God through his two incarnations, the two beasts (Ch. 13), that attack, too, is defeated. The story of the last attack and the final overthrow of the two beasts is told with almost contemptuous brevity (19:11-21); the beast and the false prophet are spoken of only in the passive voice. (19:20)

As it was at the beginning of the end, so it is at the end of the end, now in the final vision of "what must soon take place" (1:1). Once more the vision underscores the fact that the church in her agony faces a defeated enemy:

> He can harm us none;
> He's judged, the deed is done.

Satan is bound; the killer and liar (John 8:44) can really deceive and kill no more. For those who do not will to love his lie there is a resurrection even now, and there is for them even now a reign with Christ "to the close of the age" (Matt. 28:20); for a "thousand years" they are permitted to extend the reign

129

of the Lord whose resurrection they share. The ghastly semblance of resilient satanic vitality which is concentrated in the attack of Gog and Magog upon the people of God is futile, no match for the judicial vitality of the fire of God (20:9). In the Last Judgment the ancient accuser, Satan, has no voice; men are judged by what is written in the books of their liberated lives and in God's book of life. (20:12, 15)

1 "The testimony of Jesus is the spirit of prophecy" (19:10). Jesus interpreted His driving out of demons as the work of One who has bound the strong man (Beelzebul, Satan) and thus has power to invade the strong man's house and plunder it (Matt. 12:29). Similarly, the prophet John sees the final overthrow of Satan (20:10) as the ultimate effect or working-out of the judgment executed upon Satan at the beginning of the end, when Satan was rendered powerless by the coming of Christ (cf. 12:10, where the event here described as the binding of Satan is pictured as the expulsion of Satan from his place as the accuser of men, and John 12:31; Luke 10:18, where Jesus uses the same picture).

John sees a messenger of God descending from heaven. The angel is authorized to execute judgment; he holds in his hand the key to "the bottomless pit," having authority to banish thither, and having the power to bind the condemned person for consignment to that place shut out from the light and life of God (cf. 9:1, 11). 2 The condemned prisoner is the dragon, "who is the Devil and Satan," the ancient serpent, deceiver and adversary of man from the beginning (Gen. 3; John 8:44). Him the angel seizes and binds "for a thousand years." As is usual with numbers in Revelation (cf., e. g., the Spirit designated as "seven spirits," 1:4) the number "thousand" is symbolic: "Ten" is the number of the rounded whole; 10 times 10 times 10 is, then, the completely, definitively rounded whole (cf. the 12 tribes multiplied by 12 and then multiplied by the third power of 10 in the 144,000 of God's people, 7:4-8; 14:1).

3 For these "thousand years" Satan is confined to that dark abode of impotence. He has lost the aura of invincibility that was his before the Messianic Child was born. Then, he was thrust from his place as accuser, to which God's

wrath on man's sin assigned him; now that he is bound, he is seen as the pseudopower he really is, a power that can deceive only those who choose to be deceived. He is seen as *Gottes Teufel* ("God's devil," Luther); and it is God's sovereign control of history, the "must" of His will, which shall permit him to "be loosed for a little while" to make a final and futile attack upon the people of God. (cf. 20:7-10)

4 The futility of Satan's still-impending last attack (the "great tribulation" of which Jesus had spoken, Matt. 24:21) is already foretokened by the succinct description of the fate of the persecuted church given in vv. 4-6. During those "thousand years" the existence of the church has before it the key signature of "dying, and behold we live" (2 Cor. 6:9; cf. Rom. 8:37: *"In all these things* we are more than conquerors through him who loved us"). Those faithful ones who have been judged and condemned in human courts, "beheaded for their testimony to Jesus" (because they have confessed Him as the acquitting "Word of God," 19:13, which silences the voice of the accuser and makes void the claim of Antichrist to their worship and their fealty)—they are in reality not judged and condemned men but the judges; they are enthroned as judges over all the hostile powers which have, apparently, triumphed over them. In the court of God the verdict of the world is reversed; there the Spirit pleads their cause and "convinces the world concerning . . . judgment, because the ruler of this world [Satan] is judged" (John 16:8, 11). John's language recalls the description in Daniel of the judgment executed through the Son of Man upon the four beasts arising from the sea who symbolize the powers hostile to God and His people (Dan. 7:9-14). Those who have lost their lives for Christ's sake find their life (Matt. 10:39); they come to life and reign with Christ. (Cf. John 12:26)

5 Christ promised, "I am the resurrection and the life; he who believes in me, though he die, yet shall he live" (John 11:25); and He holds to His word. For those who believe in Him there is a "first resurrection," a being-raised to a life not canceled out by men's dying, a life like that of the risen Christ's, no longer exposed to death (cf. Rom. 6:9). Those who have refused to find resurrection and life in

Christ will not share in this "first resurrection" during the 1,000 years. **6** The life of those who believe in Christ "is hid with Christ in God" (Col. 3:3). The "first resurrection" is not yet manifest, but it is not for that reason merely "ideal" or "unreal." It bestows a real blessedness, the blessedness of the man who has become God's man ("holy") and is therefore removed from the power of that "second death" which is the appointed destiny of all who oppose the will and grace of God (vv. 10, 14, 15). God wills life, and God's men inherit life.

They live to share Christ's reign, these martyr-conquerors (cf. 3:21). And they use their regal power in a priestly ministry to mankind: By their Gospel witness in life and death they mediate the blessings of the Crucified and unite men with the Lord whom to serve is perfect liberty. In them the love of Him who by His blood freed men from their sins and made them kings and priests finds its final fruitage; the pronounced praise of the first doxology in Revelation (1:5-6) becomes enacted praise during the 1,000 years. Satan is bound; not the will of the liar and murderer but the will of God prevails, and that will is "grace and truth" (John 1: 14, 17). Therefore His saints live and reign, and Satan can no longer deceive the nations with his false show of power.

Extended Note: The Millennial Hope

The three verses Rev. 20:4-6 are actually the only basis for what has come to be known as millennialism (a term derived from the Latin word for "thousand years") or chiliasm (from the Greek word for "thousand," namely the expectation (in a variety of forms) "that, before the resurrection of the dead, saints and godly men will possess a worldly kingdom and annihilate all the godless" (Augsburg Confession, Article XVII). The words of our Lord, in all other respects in strong agreement with the witness of The Revelation to John, say nothing of a triumphant interregnum of Christ and His own before His final return to judge the quick and the dead and to gather His elect into glory. With this the rest of the New Testament Witnesses agree. The whole New Testament witness is not only silent as regards a millennium; rather, it excludes the idea of a millennium: according to it, the church will remain the church "hidden under the cross" to the very end, and "he who endures *to the end* will be saved" (Matt. 10:22). The Lutheran Confessions are therefore understandably brief and brusque in rejecting "certain Jewish opinions which are even now making an appearance and which teach that, before the resurrection of the dead, saints and godly men will possess a worldly kingdom and annihilate all the godless." (Augsburg Confession, Article XVII)

Those who cherish and foster the millennial hope (and these have from of old included great and good men) need to ask themselves whether the desire to have and enjoy a visible victory before the final victory of the Crucified is not a subtle and unconscious form of objection to the Crucified who unseals the scroll taken from the hand of God; He in His wisdom and power keeps the church hidden under the cross, and He has promised to be with His church, under the cross, "to the close of the age." (Matt. 28:20)

7 Even Satan's last great show of power, his frontal attack on a universal scale, is branded as a lie. It is God's will, His "must" (3), that releases Satan for his last assault at the end of the 1,000 years. God would have His people learn that they are dependent on Him all the way, to the very end, even in those thousand years; there never comes a time when man can "go it alone." Therefore He allows Satan a last attempt to rally mankind round his pseudokingship.

8 The attempt is as universal in scope as the pretensions of Satan are universal in intent; the nations inspired to opposition by his deceit are like the sand of the sea in number. The names "Gog and Magog" characterize the forces as forces which attack the people of God just when their security seems assured; Ezekiel had spoken of the last enemy of old Israel as "Gog, of the land of Magog" (Ezek. 38:2), who was to lead his hordes against Israel when Israle had been restored after the Babylonian captivity as a "people gathered from the nations ... dwelling securely" (Ezek. 38:12, 14). In Judaism "Gog" and "Magog" came to be known as two persons, enemies of the Messiah. Here in

Revelation "Gog" and "Magog" represent those satanically inspired powers in history who pit themselves against the people of God (cf. 16:12-16; 19:17-21) in a last desperate battle.

9 They advance on a worldwide front ("over the broad earth") and surround "the camp of the saints and the beloved city." "Camp" recalls Israel during the wanderings in the wilderness (Ex. *passim*; cf. Rev. 12:14), while "the beloved city" recalls the time when Israel had found a land and rest in Canaan. Even in the thousand years the church remains a pilgrim people who have not yet found a "lasting city" (Heb. 13:14); the "lasting city," no longer liable to attack, will be theirs at the end of days on God's new earth under His new-created heaven (21:1-2). The massive and concerted attack headed by Gog and Magog comes to nothing. As in the case of Gog in the prophecy of Ezekiel (Ezek. 39:6), fire from heaven executes God's judgment upon His enemies. (Some ancient authorities have the reading "fire *from God,* out of heaven," which is a true interpretation of the text even though it can hardly lay claim to being the original reading.)

10 Both the deceived and the deceiver receive their due reward. The deceived are consumed by fire, and the devil who had deceived them is consigned (together with his already-judged agents, the first and second beast) to everlasting torment in that "eternal fire prepared for the devil and his angels" of which Jesus had spoken (Matt. 25:41), here called "the lake of fire and brimstone." Thus ends the history of that proud spirit who for so long had both deceived and terrified mankind.

The Last Judgment
20:11-15

Babylon, the first and second beast, and Satan himself have been judged and destroyed. On the deeper level of the subsurface reality of the battle between God and His enemies (cf. the comments immediately preceding 12:1), the decisive deed is done; the way is clear for the coming of God's kingdom and the appearance of His new world in new glory (21:1—22:5). But at the level of surface reality there remains the last judgment on men in which God will purge from mankind all those who have not heeded the warnings uttered by the seals, trumpets, and bowls of God's visitations and have not listened to the eternal Gospel of His call to repentance (14:6-7). There remains the judgment on those who have not repented and have not prayed and striven for the hallowing of His name, the coming of His kingdom, and the being-done of His will. This last judgment is the subject of the prophet's vision in 20:11-15.

11 The prophet sees again (cf. 4:2) the enthroned King whose hands have held the reins of all history, "the Lord God Almighty, who was and is and is to come" (4:8), seated on a great white throne. White is the color of final, heavenly fulfillment; and He to whom judgment belongs is seated on *this* throne in sole sovereignty. Before Him the old earth and sky, marred by man's sin (cf. Rom. 8:20) and defaced by satanic revolt, cannot stand; they flee away, to give place to a new heaven and a new earth transfigured by the Creator's hand and made fit to stand before Him, "very good" (Gen. 1:31) once more.

12 From His judgment there is no escape, even in death:

If I make my bed in Sheol, thou art there! (Ps. 139:8)

Men may cry for annihilation by appealing to the mountains and rocks for covering refuge from His requiting presence (6:16-17), but to no avail. No man is so great that he can defy His judgment, and no man is so small that he may hope to be ignored. All men must stand and give an account before Him whose remembering judgment has recorded all men's deeds. All are "judged by what was written in the books, by what they had done." But God's remembering mercy remains active and effective for men in the midst of judgment; He remembers that their names are inscribed in His "book of life," that He has enrolled them as citizens of His heavenly city, that He has loved and chosen them from everlasting—the record of "what they had done" is no mere impersonal set of statistics on their autonomous acts, but the record of their created response to His elective love, the record of a life lived under the heaven of their Father's forgiveness (cf. Matt. 6:12). It is worth noting that Revelation mentions the books only here, while "the book of life" occurs six times (cf. 3:5; 13:8; 17:8; 20:12, 15; 21:27). Just so Jesus in His portrayal of the Last Judgment spoke not only of what men had done or left undone, prominent and important though the deeds of men are in His portrayal; He pictures the Son of Man, the King, as summoning to Himself and to eternal life men for whom God has prepared the blessing of the inheritance of His kingdom before any willing or running of man, "from the foundation of the world" (Matt. 25:34). **13** Life, eternal life, is God's will for man, as is apparent from the book of life. Therefore men drowned at sea are not forgotten wreckage; the sea gives up its dead.

14 Death and Hades, though used by God as executors of His purpose (6:8) and allowed for a space to range in the world, are not permitted to range forever. They have finished their part in the divine drama and are now dismissed and destroyed, consigned to the lake of fire which is the fate of all who speak a satanic No to the life willed by God—"Death, thou shalt die!" **15** That satanic No to God's will of life is a fearful thing; it can erase a man's name from the book of life and commit him to "the eternal fire" which God has not willed for man but has "prepared for the devil and his angels" (Matt. 25:41). "The hour is coming, and now is," Jesus said (John 5:25). The hour is coming when God's will of life will be victoriously manifested; the hour now is when man speaks, by what he has done, his Yes or his No to that will.

The New World of God: Creation
21:1-8

In His wrath upon man in revolt against Him God has harried and scourged the world created for man (cf., e. g., 8:7-11); the earth and sky disfigured by satanic revolt and human sin have had to flee from the presence of God the Judge, who will not tolerate the marring of His creation (20:11; cf. 11:18). But He is not minded to annihilate the "very good" creation which once He hallowed with His blessing (Gen. 1). Likewise, God's response to man's defiance of Him in his allegiance to dark powers has been stark and unsparing judgmental visitation; the opening of the seven seals, the sounding of the seven trumpets, and the emptying of the seven bowls of wrath testify to that. But He has not renounced His ancient purpose that man should live in communion with Him; the Lord God Almighty has always, in the midst of judgment, a rainbow round His throne (4:3), and the angels who pour out on mankind the seven bowls of the wrath of God subserve God's will to communion with man: They proceed from "the temple of the tent of witness" (15:5-8), the olden symbol of God's presence among His people, and their visitations are designed to turn men to the God who smites them for their good. (16:9, 11; cf. Amos 4:6-11)

This crowning vision of Revelation (21:1—22:5) is therefore both a song of creation, celebrating the making-new of heaven and earth, and a song of redemption, celebrating the consummated communion between God and man in His holy city, new Jerusalem, significantly named the bride of the Lamb who by His sacrifice has freed men from their sins (1:5-6) and made them capable of communion with God (cf. Eph. 5:25-27). This ancient twin theme of God the Creator and Redeemer (cf., e. g., Is. 42:5-9; 44:24-28), a theme already announced in the vision of Chs. 4 and 5 (cf. 4:11; 5:9-14), receives its full climactic treatment here.

1 "New" is the characteristic adjective of the ultimate creation as it is the characteristic of the whole of Revelation. The saints of God will bear their new name, Christ's own name (2:17; 3:12), and sing unendingly their new song (14:3) in a world where God makes all things new (21:5), on a new earth and under a new heaven, in a new holy city, a new Jerusalem. All things are "new," not merely as more recent in date but as created and designed to supresede and replace the old, the "first"—new with an astonishing end-of-time newness, unheard-of and wondrous, as unpredictably strange as the fact that the new covenant which succeeds and replaces the ruins of the guilt-marred old covenant should be a covenant of divine forgiveness, which renews

men for knowledge of God and for a spontaneous obedience to Him (Jer. 31:31-34; Luke 22:20; 1 Cor. 11:25). The "new heaven and new earth" supersede and replace the "first," those witnesses and victims of the cosmic ruin and futility brought upon the world by man's first disobedience (Rom. 8:20). In this new world the sea, the uncanny remnant of primeval chaos from which satanic powers can arise to mislead mankind (cf. 13:1), shall be no more.

2 There shall be nothing to divide man from man or man from God. For there shall be created a "new Jerusalem" as God's gift to man. As the old Jerusalem, seat of the Lord's anointed king and site of the Lord's temple, was the focus of God's will-to-communion with His people and had upon it the promise of a still greater communion with all mankind (cf. Is. 2:1-4; Micah 4:1-7; Is. 56:7), so the new holy city shall be. She is portrayed as splendidly decked out, prepared for the closest communion known to human experience, the connubial communion between man and woman. She is "the Bride, the wife of the Lamb." (9)

3 A "loud voice from the throne" spells out what "Jerusalem" means: "Jerusalem" means that God is present with His peoples (the plural is significant, and the reading of footnote *o* is to be preferred; God in the new world is not "the God of Jews only" (Rom. 3:29), but God of all peoples, present as their God.

4 He will fulfill the promise of Is. 25:8 that the Lord God would "swallow up death for ever" and would "wipe away tears from all faces." On that day His people may well say, "Lo, this is our God; we have waited for him . . . let us be glad and rejoice in his salvation" (Is. 25:9), for death with all its consequences ("mourning," "crying") and antecedents ("pain"), all that made "the former things" a sad history of the reign of death (Rom. 5:17, 21), will be no more.

5 Are such high promises believable for man living in this world? Are they believable, above all, for the tried and dying church? Here (and here only in Revelation), where the promise is most extravagant, God Himself is introduced as speaking. He who once "spoke, and it came to be," at the first creation (Ps. 33:9), now speaks again, affirming His final creative work and assuring the afflicted prophet of the suffering church (cf. 1:9) that the words the prophet is empowered to utter are a divine word, to be trusted and believed.

6 When God speaks, His speaking is an accomplished deed; with Him there is no gap between promise and fulfillment, for in the alphabet of the world's history He is the first letter ("the Alpha") and the last ("the Omega"), cf. 1:8. His will controlled the beginning, and it controls the end. And that will is grace. To those who are thirsty, to those who need Him and are dying in their need, He gives—with a free generosity that is measured only by their need of Him—the life-giving waters which only He can give. (Cf. Ps. 36:9)

7 In the words which the Spirit spoke to the churches in the seven letters (Chs. 2—3) each word concludes with a promise to the "conqueror" (2:7, 11, 17, 26; 3:5, 12, 21); all those promises are gathered into one when God here proffers to the conqueror "this heritage." The conqueror shall receive no less than was promised to the Messiah (2 Sam. 7:13, 16; cf. Ps. 89:26-27). In Rev. 3:21 the Spirit promised to the conqueror coenthronement on the Father's throne with Christ; here God promises to the conqueror the gift of Himself and the place and privilege of a son of God.

8 The promise holds for all who will enter upon this freely given heritage, for all who will enter upon Christ's victory and thus receive it as their own. Those who in faithless cowardice (cf. 2 Tim. 1:7) shrink from the cross of martyrdom forfeit the crown. They void the promise given them, those who belie the promise by polluting themselves with the "abominations" of the harlot Babylon (17:4). The verb "pollute" belongs to the same word family as the noun "abomination." They void the promise, those who by murdering the saints help make the harlot "drunk with the blood of the saints and the blood of the martyrs of Jesus" (17:6), those who drink from Babylon's golden cup "full of . . . . the impurities of her fornication" (17:4), all those who replace the true awe-filled worship of the Creator of heaven and earth (cf. 14:7) with the bold satanic lie of sorcery and idolatry. Their fealty is a fealty to Satan, and they make Satan's destiny their own; their place shall be in the fire prepared for Satan and his servitors, the unceasing torture of the lake of fire, the dark second death lit by no hope of resurrection.

The New World of God: Redemption
21:9—22:5

9 God is working out His purposes; His purpose has never been that man should perish with the enemy of God and man. Even the seven angels who poured out His seven last plagues upon the world served God's saving purpose. And even though one of those angels climaxed his ministry by revealing the judgment on Babylon (17:1), it is one of those same angels who reveals to the prophet the final fate of the church, the new Jerusalem. She is in all things the very antithesis of the harlot, that creature of wild unbridled passion without ties and loyalties. She is the creature whom God created for Himself, united with God by her marriage (she is now called not only "bride" but "wife" also) to the Lamb of God who died to set her free to be His own. (1:5-6; cf. Eph. 5:25-27)

10 That is the inner beauty of the new Jerusalem, her complete communion with her Lord. To this her external beauty corresponds; the Spirit makes visible to the prophet from afar (from "a great high mountain") the beauty which no eye of man can see (cf. 1 Cor. 2:9). Jerusalem is a "holy city," God's own creation coming down from heaven, the domain of God. **11** She is therefore bright with God's own glory, with the radiance of His manifested holiness (cf. Is. 60:1-3). Only the rarest and brightest of created things, a jewel "like a jasper" but crystal-clear and translucent, can serve as a comparison for this glory.

12-13 The new Jerusalem is a plant of heaven, but it has long ago struck roots on earth. The number "twelve" occurring three times in one verse in the description of the city recalls the first striking-root of God's plant in "the twelve tribes of the sons of Israel." From that unpromising beginning has come this high-walled radiant fortress with its 12 gates guarded by 12 angels, as impregnable as it is bright, for all that the 12 gates open in all directions to all the world. **14** The roots struck in Israel have spread to all the world; the 12 foundation-stones have inscribed on them the "names of the twelve apostles of the Lamb," the messengers sent by the risen Christ to all nations. (Matt. 28:19)

> Walk about Zion, go round about her,
> number her towers,
> consider well her ramparts,
> go through her citadels;
> that you may tell the next generation
> that this is God,
> our God for ever and ever. (Ps. 48:12-14)

In the spirit of Ps. 48 the vision lingers lovingly over the details of the dimensions and materials of the holy city, the place where God manifests Himself as "our God for ever and ever." **16** The city as measured by the angel with his golden measuring rod lay foursquare, its breadth equal to its length, like the court of the new temple which Ezekiel once beheld (Ezek. 40:47). The idea of the foursquare perfection of the huge city is carried even further in the notice that the city is a great cube. (Cf. the cubic shape of the inner sanctuary of Solomon's temple, 1 Kings 6:20.)

17 The "great high wall" (12) seems, in comparison with the other dimensions, strangely small (only 216 feet high). The dimension is symbolic rather than descriptive. The number 144 is one of the many multiples of 12 which abound in the description of the city as the home of the enlarged 12 tribes, and the puny scale of the wall indicates that it serves not as a defense (since all God's enemies lie conquered) but merely as a delimiting enclosure. The slightness of the wall is emphasized by the prophet's notation that the cubits are "man's measure" (the ordinary 18 inches, not some fantastic "angelic" measurement). The angels, as fellow servants of the prophets (19:10; 22:9), use the measures of men.

18 Though the wall is slight, it is precious and splendid, built of the jasper which serves as a picture of the effulgent glory of God (cf. 11). And the city itself is a city of gold strangely and wondrously pellucid. **19-21** The whole structure of the city is adazzle with the brilliance and color of gems and gold, its foundations adorned with the jewels that once were set in gold filigree in the high priest's breastpiece

141

(Ex. 28:17-20), its 12 gates each a single pearl, its street of shimmering transparent gold. The details in the identification of the 12 gems are uncertain (some scholars call attention to an ancient correlation between the gems of the high priest's breastpiece and the signs of the zodiac), but there can be no doubt about the oriental rich splendor of the whole.

22 John's vision of the new Jerusalem is a song of the communion between God and man: "The dwelling of God is with men" (3). There is therefore no temple of God in the city. The presence of God is no longer mediated by a temple; His presence in overwhelming power and in astonishing grace is an immediate presence.

23 Before that light-giving presence the great lights of the first creation (Gen. 1:14-19) grow pale and meaningless, like our lamps at sunrise. God's glory, manifested in the Lamb (cf. John 1:4), is now wholly and forever "the light of the world." (John 8:12)

24 The light of the world is the life of the world. By it men of all nations may walk, healthy and alive. Their walking is an enacted doxology to the God who has shined into their darkness. The greatest men of the nations bring home with them all the gifts of wealth and power which have made them great. **25-26** The 12 gates are open to receive "the glory and the honor of the nations" as the nations, no longer aliens and enemies, offer willing tribute to their God; whatever His sovereign control of all histories and all cultures has brought forth that is splendid and honorable will come home to Him and will be forever kept safe in His city. No one can imperil His gathered treasures; therefore the gates are never shut by day—and there is no more night in which thieves may break in and steal.

27 Nothing unclean will be permitted to sully the clean holiness of the city; he who has excluded himself from God by the lie of false worship will be excluded from the city of God. Only those whose names have been inscribed by the Lamb's redeeming love in the citizens' roll of the new Jerusalem shall live there.

22:1 They shall *live* there, not merely dwell there; for in the city where God and the Lamb are enthroned there is divine life. In this paradise restored "the water of life" flows in sparkling vitality "from the throne," **2** and by that river grows the paradisal tree of life, bringing forth fruit with exuberant fertility. Man, cured at last of his imperious self-seeking, is no longer excluded from it by the flaming sword of the cherubim (Gen. 3:22-24). Its leaves will heal the hurt of all the nations gathered thither; the healing ministry of Jesus of Nazareth, who once "went about doing good" in one small corner of the world (Acts 10:38), will reach its universal climax there.

3 The graciously regnant presence of God and the Lamb will cancel the ancient curse which has blighted the ground (Gen. 3:17) and will make the earth God's earth and the ground man's ground again. The martyred servants of God will no longer cry out in desperation amid a dying for His sake which they cannot understand (6:10). Set free for their proper work of worship, **4** they shall see the face of Him who loved them, as Jesus had promised to the pure in heart (Matt. 5:8). The name of the Lord who loved them and ransomed them will be inscribed on their foreheads and will mark as His own forever those who never accepted the mark of the beast. (13:16)

5 "Let there be light," God's first word at creation, will be His last word too. The Lord Himself will be the answer to His primeval command; and in that light, which makes all other lights superfluous, the servants of God shall live and reign forever.

Epilog
22:6-21

The Revelation to John closes with a series of utterances, by various voices, which mark the book as the *prophetic* word that it claims to be (1:3; 22:7, 9, 10, 16, 18, 19). The utterances are all characterized by a prophetic sense of urgency and by a prophetic moral and religious earnestness. All the voices, varied as they are (whether Christ's, the prophet's, the angel's, or the voice of the Spirit and the Bride), are at one in insisting that the book is not a human word to be admired or even to be altered by men, but an inspired word to be heard and kept (1:3) no matter at what cost.

6 The first voice once more assures the prophet that the words he has been authorized to write to the churches are "trustworthy and true" (cf. 21:5), as Christ Himself is trustworthy and true (cf. 3:14; 19:11). The Lord who inspired His prophets of old to see the invisible and to speak the ineffable is the Author of the visions of John in the last urgent days before His return. **7** The closing words of the first voice, "I am coming soon," make it clear that it is the voice of the returning Lord Himself (cf. 3:11; 16:15; 22:12, 20). It is He who at the close once more pronounces the beatitude heard at the beginning. (1:3)

8 Again (cf. 19:10) the prophet is so overwhelmed by what he hears and sees that he falls at the feet of the angel who mediated the word and the vision in order to pay him divine honors. **9** Again the angel checks the prophet's impulse to worship him, puts himself on a level with the speakers and hearers of the prophetic word, and bids the prophet worship Him to whom alone all worship is due.

10 He who comes quickly, the returning Christ Himself, speaks again. He forbids the prophet to do what the prophet Daniel in his day had been bidden to do, to seal up the words of prophecy and so reserve his word for some far-off future day (Dan. 8:26; 12:4). John's day is not the same as Daniel's day, and John's word in his day is to be heard at once while there is yet time. **11** Now all men, the evildoer, the filthy, the righteous, the holy, are to hear and know whither they are moving, whether in their filthiness or in their holiness; the times of ignorance are past.

12 All men are moving, not toward a distant, dimly apprehended future but toward Him who draws near soon, to judge and to reward. The high majesty of the approaching Judge is suggested by the fact that this language is reminiscent of the language of the Lord God in Is. 40:10; **13** the high majesty is explicitly asserted in the coming Judge's claim to be "the Alpha and the Omega . . . the beginning and the end," elsewhere attributes of God Himself (1:8; 21:6). The evildoer and the filthy, the righteous and the holy, will be exposed to the judicial scrutiny of One who is Author of all creation and of all history and the appointed Goal and Judge of all history (cf. Col. 1:15-16; Acts 17:31), and each will be repaid by Him for what he individually has done.

14 The laconic imperatives of v. 11 are anything but a cool deterministic forecast of what will happen; they are a call to repentance and so, indirectly, an invitation to taste and see what blessed things may yet happen. The blessed future of the new Jerusalem reaches effectively into the present and fills the present with its unheard-of possibilities. Men may *now* wash their filthy robes white in the atoning blood of the Lamb (cf. 7:14), may now be clothed in garments of salvation that qualify them for their final priestly worship "before the throne of God" (7:15; cf. 21:3-4). The healing and health of the tree of life (cf. 22:2) may become theirs now; the splendid gates of the new Jerusalem are opening for them even now. **15** Only the hard will of impenitence will close those gates forever; only those who choose to cast in their lot with the impure ("the dogs," unclean animals, used of Sodomites, Deut. 23:18), only those who love and practice the lie of antichristian idolatry ("sorcerers," etc., cf. comments on 21:8), fall under the imprecation which commits them to the outer darkness ("outside," cf. Matt. 8:12; 22:13).

16 It is Jesus, the pure Man (1 Peter 2:22-23) who loved His God with all His heart and would worship no other (Matt. 4:10), who thus seeks, by promise and threat, to win men to Himself and to His future. He antedates our human history, for He is the divine "root," the archetypal royal Source, from which the Messiah sprang. He has entered our history as "the offspring of David" (cf. Rom. 1:3). The one Man who has a future, the Morning Star (cf. Num. 24:17) who ushers in God's eternal day, has in this Revelation to John been inviting men into His future.

17 The Spirit moves the church on earth (here significantly called "Bride," though that term has hitherto been reserved for the glorified church of the world to come) to enter by prayer upon that future event now. We are present now, it seems, at the church's celebration of the Lord's Supper, where past, present, and future overlap and coalesce, and we hear the eucharistic cry of "Maranatha!" (1 Cor. 16:22, note *c*). In this cry all who hear are invited to join; and all who desire "the water of life," which is the gift of God and the Lamb to the new Jerusalem (cf. 1), are invited to take now the life-giving water now being proffered freely. When men have learned so to pray and have heeded the invitation to take the water of life, John's book has accomplished its purpose.

18-19 The purpose is God's own purpose. John has in calling his book a book of prophecy (1:3) affixed to it the seal of "Thus says the Lord," by implication at least. Now he expressly affirms the sanctity of the book as word of God by making God the jealous Guardian of its sanctity, the Guardian who will brook no additions to or any diminution of what His word declares and bestows. The curses and blessings of the book are not inert literary data but the "living and active" (Heb. 4:12) word of God which will avenge itself on all who desecrate its sanctity.

20 Jesus, "the faithful witness" (1:5), confirms the sanctity of the book by once more asserting the urgency of its message: "Surely I am coming soon." His servant the prophet responds to that promise of grace with the church's prayer for the ultimate grace, "Come, Lord Jesus!"

21 This aspect of grace as the ultimate grace surely colors also the use of "grace" in the closing epistolary benediction. The grace which the prophet invokes upon all the saints at the end of his long letter (cf. comments on 1:4) is the grace for which the church prays in the post-Communion prayer found in the second-century *Teaching of the Twelve Apostles:* "Let grace come, and let the world pass away."

146

For Further Reading

Morris, Leon. *The Revelation of St. John,* The Tyndale New Testament Commentaries. London: The Tyndale Press, 1969.

This commentary, moderate in length (263 pages) and modest in price, fulfills admirably the announced purpose of the Tyndale series (p. 5): to provide commentaries "which avoid the extremes of being unduly technical or unhelpfully brief." The commentary is based on the Authorized Version, but later versions are included in the discussion, "to show why, on textual and linguistic grounds, the later versions are so often to be preferred" (p. 5). The commentary is reverent, sober, and thoughtful. The introduction (pp. 15—41) provides in brief compass reliable information and well-considered judgment on Interpretation, The Revelation of St. John and Apocalyptic, Authorship, Date, and Sources. There is no formal bibliography; but between the list of Chief Abbreviations (pp. 9—12) and the notices in the commentary itself, the reader will find considerable guidance for further reading in books on and about The Revelation to John.

Caird, G. B. *A Commentary on the Revelation of St. John the Divine.* Black's New Testament Commentaries. London: Adam and Charles Black, 1966. (In the U.S.A.: Harper's New Testament Commentaries. New York and Evanston: Harper and Row.)

In this commentary, somewhat more technical and fuller than that of Morris (301 pages), the author provides his own translation of the Greek text and a lucid and original interpretation of the text. Noteworthy are (A) his efforts to understand the text as it stands (he rides no theories and constructs no hypotheses); (B) his understanding of the practical relevance of The Revelation to John, in keeping with his purpose "to help the reader put himself in the place of the Asiatic Christians of the first century . . . so that he may hear what the Spirit was then saying to the churches, and also be better able to hear what the Spirit is saying to the churches of our own day"; (C) his appreciation and understanding of the artistry of John, both in the structure of the book as a whole and in matters of detail; (D) his theological understanding of, and stress on, the character of the book as a continuation of the Gospel of the Crucified. A closing chapter (pp. 289—301) on "The Theology of the Book of Revelation" is lucid and helpful on this point. One is inclined to place question marks in the margin at points (e. g., p. 191) where the cast shadow of the Gospel, the wrath of God and of the Lamb, is unduly played down.

There is a brief bibliography, which includes books in French and German. And there are two indexes, one of Biblical References and another of Non-Biblical References.